CHASING SOPHIA

RECLAIMING THE LOST WISDOM OF JESUS

Lilian Calles Barger

JB JOSSEY-BASS

1807
WILEY
2007
BICENTENNIAL

Published by Jossey-Bass
A Wiley Imprint
989 Market Street, San Francisco, CA 94103-1741   www.josseybass.com

Jossey-Bass books and products are available through most bookstores. To contact Jossey-Bass directly, call our Customer Care Department within the U.S. at 800-956-7739, outside the U.S. at 317-572-3986, or fax 317-572-4002.

Jossey-Bass also publishes its books in a variety of electronic formats. Some content that appears in print may not be available in electronic books.

Credits are on page 250.

Library of Congress Cataloging-in-Publication Data
Barger, Lilian Calles.
   Chasing Sophia: reclaiming the lost wisdom of Jesus / Lilian Calles Barger.
      p. cm.
   Includes bibliographical references and index.
   ISBN-13: 978-0-7879-8380-2 (pbk.)
   ISBN-10: 0-7879-8380-2 (pbk.)
   1. God (Christianity)—Wisdom. 2. Femininity of God. 3. Jesus Christ. 4. Wisdom (Biblical personification) 5. Wisdom—Religious aspects—Christianity. I. Title.
   BT150.B37 2007
   230.082—dc22   2006035833

Printed in the United States of America
FIRST EDITION

PB Printing   10 9 8 7 6 5 4 3 2 1

CONTENTS

ACKNOWLEDGMENTS

I am indebted to many people who have supported the writing of this book. I would especially like to thank my agent, Leslie Nunn Reed, for sticking with me, my first reader, Rhonda Teel Gray, for taking the brunt of reading raw pages of manuscript, and my editors Marcia Ford and Julianna Gustafson at Jossey-Bass for their insight and sensitivity and for helping me be a better writer.

I would also like to thank my coworker at the Damaris Project—Jodi Teal—for championing the ideas in this book. Thank you to the entire board of the Damaris Project, which includes Melissa Young, Paula Mann, and Suzy Renz, as well as my friends Angela Morrison, Sallie Clingman, and Katina Simmons.

Last, but certainly not least, thank you to my gracious husband, David Barger, for supporting me on another wild adventure.

In memory of my father, Ruben Francisco Calles

CHASING SOPHIA

If you are wise, your wisdom will reward you;
if you are a mocker, you alone will suffer.

PROVERBS 9:12

WHO NEEDS SOPHIA?

At thirty-four, knee-deep in life, I concluded I was too young to write the one book I thought I had in me. At that point, I could feel my conclusions about life welling up inside me, screaming to be heard. Because I didn't trust my own knowledge, I wasn't sure if what I had to say was worth saying.

The freedom to write or not write quickly became a metaphor for my relationship with the world. I was left with a deep-seated urge to speak, to say something, even though I was not sure what. That same year my second son was born, and after my own life-threatening encounter with toxic shock, I was forced to rethink my life. Between the prospects of dying or living, I wanted to live, and living came to mean one thing to me—having a voice that could be heard to the hills. What I knew intuitively was waiting to come out of the silence. In order to say what I knew out loud, I would have to embrace my own experiences and give them words. However, I was held back by a plague of self-doubt that I believed was a hazard of my temperament. It took me ten years to get comfortable with my own voice and to write my first book.

Along the way to developing self-assurance, I talked to women of all ages who reflected my own hesitation to commit to what they knew—about themselves, about the world, and even about God. I was not alone. Bright and accomplished women of all ages found themselves clueless in so many areas of their lives. The tentativeness these women felt sent many on a spiritual quest into uncharted territory. What we were all seeking was a place where we could speak and act out of our most authentic selves. I call that place wisdom. Wisdom seeking in modern society is no easy task, particularly for women. Attempting to unearth the wisdom tradition from years of neglect would take me to places I wasn't sure I wanted to go, crossing the path of other women who were making their own way to wise knowing.

I saw that underneath the search for wisdom was a deep doubt about God and a spiritual foundation that can no longer support life. With my share of successes (and failures), no one would ever describe me as lacking in self-confidence or as having an insecure faith. I haven't spent my life sitting on my hands. Nevertheless, finding a coherent life from which I can finally speak and act out of a deep confidence has been difficult. This book is for all those women who, like me, seek a kind of wisdom that will allow us to own our faith and to live with confidence.

The search for my own spiritual voice and knowing quickly became a journey toward a renewed faith in Jesus.

This journey required that I unpack the bundle of beliefs about God and women that I inherited. I had to question what I was given by my family, my church, and my culture. As a follower of Jesus from a very young age, I had to face my own faith community's role in fostering women's self-doubt. Why did the Christian religious experience often feel disempowering to me and other women I knew? I also had to understand that any faith tradition, as much as it leaves its own mark on a culture, is also shaped by its surrounding culture.

In contemporary society, the search for wisdom as a basic human pursuit has gotten seriously sidetracked. The early Christians' vibrant and central understanding of Jesus as the Wisdom of God has been virtually forgotten, except for what remains in the pages of dusty theology books and the hopeful glimmers in the Eastern Orthodox tradition. The fullness and richness of the idea of Jesus as the Wisdom of God has been lost for centuries and lost on us. But wisdom is not a purely religious idea. From ancient times wisdom has presented itself in many disguises: literary, artistic, or philosophical—even as everyday common sense. For centuries it has been pursued, collected, tried, and passed on by ordinary people.

In the chapters that follow, I will explore the need for the ancient idea of wisdom and how it might possibly serve us now. I will follow the path cleared by women who have gone before us and those today who are attempting to reclaim wisdom as their own. This is why *sophia*—the feminine Greek word for wisdom—is a fitting motif for this book. For those seeking to find their female voice, *sophia* has not remained merely a Greek word for wisdom. Borrowing from ancient images of wisdom as a woman, *sophia* becomes Sophia—a feminine, divine being. I discovered that the early Christian understanding of Jesus, as the Sophia of God, needs to be dusted off from centuries of neglect and reclaimed and reimagined as an emotionally and spiritually powerful image. As a wisdom seeker and a lifelong follower of Jesus, I also recognized the need to untangle the meaning of Sophia.

In exploring our cultural understanding of wisdom, I will bring out women's often-problematic relationship to it. Women experience the pursuit of wisdom in their own unique ways. Among different cultures, women have historically been a symbol of wisdom but are often curiously denied access to it. To see women as wisdom bearers, we have to unravel centuries of often unspoken understanding about women's relation to rationality and intuition. For contemporary women, acquiring wisdom promises to disrupt dysfunctional patterns of relating to the world. For any person, the acquisition of wisdom promises to help us unmask the world, to see it for what it is, and to recognize the wisdom already in it.

In writing a book about the search for wisdom, a natural trepidation sets in. I didn't want to create the impression that I saw myself as wise and therefore ready to dispense sage advice. The spirit of the book demands that I forgo setting myself up as an expert (it's the feeling of lack that usually moves us to seek wisdom). For me to commit to writing about wisdom, I had to open myself to recognize the lack of it in my own life.

One of the first challenges I faced was the incredible wealth of wisdom literature that has accumulated through history. Philosophers, theologians, poets, artists, and many others have taken on the study of wisdom, from the esoteric to the practical. All the great world religions have a wisdom tradition. To just scratch the surface of this body of knowledge would require more than a lifetime of reflection. What I am doing is committing myself to my own life-tested conclusion about wisdom and to understanding its significance for us today.

In Chapter One, I will explore how women's search for wisdom is driving the reemergence of powerful images of the feminine divine. Chapter Two will show how our expert-driven society breeds self-doubt at virtually every turn. Chapter Three will look at the historical roots of how intuition and rationality are viewed in relation to women. In Chapter Four we'll go back to the Genesis story to find the original sources of wisdom given to us by our Creator. In Chapter Five we'll look at how Jesus established a wisdom community and how the Bible becomes its story. Chapter Six will explore the possibility of finding wisdom within ourselves, free of communal dictates. In Chapter Seven we'll look at some women who displayed wisdom through word and action, and in the final chapter we'll look at the possibility for a future full of wise individuals—and societies.

As we explore what it means to be on this journey toward wise knowing, we may just find relief from the self-doubt that plagues so many of us. The implication for our world is that the dearth of wisdom can be filled. To get us to a place of wise knowing, I will explore how wisdom encompasses multiple ways of knowing, and I will show what our bodies and the earth can teach us about wisdom and the role our communities play in the knowing process. Along the way I will look to Jesus as the embodiment of Divine Wisdom and to his teaching as a guide for our journey. In chasing Sophia we may find ourselves with the power to speak and act as true spiritual knowers and in relationship to God. Only then will many of us consider ourselves to be truly wise.

Come and eat my bread, drink the wine which I have
drawn! Leave foolishness behind and live.

PROVERBS 9:5–6

I

SOPHIA REAWAKENED

One spring I found myself with nine hundred women at a spiritual weekend of lectures, music, dance, and ritual. This was my first opportunity to gather with women who were questioning "patriarchal Christianity." I never imagined it would become a life-changing spiritual event. I was in the early stages of my journey toward understanding my faith as a woman. Up to that point, I had only a vague idea of who these women were and what they were rallying against. I had a similarly vague notion of women's low status in the church and the general absence of the female voice in theology. I was aware of the institutional battle regarding women, but I had never grappled with it myself.

Here for the first time, I heard women who considered themselves Christian naming the many wrongs done to women in the name of God and refusing to suffer in silence any longer. Here I was faced with women claiming their own knowledge of God. Through informal conversation, I heard of the wounding many had suffered in the church and at the hands of those with institutional power. In a sense, these were spiritual refugees, seeking to escape the internalized slave master, and this revival camp meeting had been conceived as a way of providing some relief from the weight of their chains.

The women I saw were a distinctly different lot from most of the women I had encountered, sitting quietly in church pews. I was used to women who continually checked their comments lest they be labeled a feminist, or worse. The women at this event, however, were strong, loud, and angry. They didn't care what men thought. I unexpectedly caught myself cheering them on at times. For the most part, though, I was filled with profound sadness over what often sounded like an exaggeration of women's experience in too many churches. It all seemed like a huge misunderstanding. Surely this would blow over, and the church and these women would find common ground and settle back into the coziness of the tradition. I was wrong.

These women felt betrayed by the institutional church and saw the very nature and basis of the Christian faith as a hindrance to their liberation. In workshop after workshop, we were challenged to do theology for ourselves and to "tell the truth" by being more honest about our lives. We were encouraged to "trouble the waters" of a patriarchal system and to reimagine the faith. The theology presented included substituting, if not completely replacing, Jesus with Sophia—the feminine personification of the Greek word for wisdom. This was a seemingly more appropriate image of the Divine for women to embrace. Sophia was blessed and worshiped in emotionally laden prayer and song. This was the first time I had heard of wisdom being used in this way.

These women had a new vision for Christianity—a vision that pushed me to rethink everything I had come to believe about God. In this new Christianity, the Jesus I knew was seldom mentioned, and when he was, he was unrecognizable. He had been fashioned into an updated feminist version and severed from two thousand years of church history. And when I say "church," I don't mean a particular denomination or institution but rather the history of millions of ordinary people who have believed that Jesus was "God with us" and have lived their lives based on that belief. This estrangement of Jesus from the living tradition made him nothing more than a myth with a political function for whoever wanted to claim him. Instead of a divine Savior, all that remained was a quintessential feminist—the Alan Alda of the cosmos. The reinterpretation of Jesus at this gathering left me shell-shocked and deeply wounded. It made me wonder whether this was Christianity at all.

Three days of reimagining, reinterpreting, and rereading Christianity left me in a personal crisis. I remained deeply unsettled for months. What these women claimed to have experienced seemed like a different religion from mine. Yet at the same time, I knew that many of their claims were true. I could readily identify with much of what they said. I had seen many friends unable to make a meaningful connection with Christianity. Yes, it mattered that women have often not fared well within the institutional structures and in theology. It's true that women haven't had the same opportunity as men to contribute to our collective understanding of God, and much injustice has been perpetrated in the name of Jesus. I felt as though my integrity was at stake. Could I honestly defend Christianity? I was left to sort out what had happened in a way that would allow me to hold on to the faith *and* live with integrity as a woman.

SHAKEN TO THE CORE

I left this gathering shaken to my core and overwrought with questions. Is Christianity inherently patriarchal? Is the feminine voice lost in the community of the Father, Son, and Holy Spirit? Would Sophia (or any feminine name for God) rescue us from what appeared to be two thousand years of silence? I had to admit that I needed to further explore this part of my experience. Many women see Sunday morning as a male parade with hardly a female voice to be heard. I became uncomfortably aware that this was true in my own church at the time. Was the group at this gathering a tiny minority of disgruntled women to be quickly forgotten, or were they functioning as a prophetic voice, pushing all women to recognize their marginal positions? Had we all been duped into making punch and serving cookies?

This is how I began a precarious—some would say dangerous—journey to discover for myself whether the faith that had been handed down to me was really a tool to keep me quiet, powerless, and clueless. I wasn't sure of the outcome. Did I dare think about these questions or risk asking them out loud? Would entertaining these questions affect my marriage and relationship to my faith community? Then the biggest question of all: Would Jesus go with me if I ventured out on my own? With these questions, I began my tour of women's spirituality.

Since then I have attended numerous conferences, gatherings, small-group circles, and various and assorted events where women were "celebrated" and encouraged to define their spiritual traditions in more feminine ways. Christianity seems to have women coming and going. I dove into theology and scoured church history for signs of female life, trying to make sense of it all. I read everything I could get my hands on, but in my immediate faith community I found myself alone. Aside from my naturally sympathetic husband, nobody in close proximity to me seemed to have a bit of trouble with the spiritual silencing of women.

As I went out looking for answers, I did not have to go very far to conclude that Father-God language is a problem for many. Feminist theologian Mary Daly's much-quoted statement says it best: "If God is male, then male is God." The conclusion is that women will not advance as long as a male God continues to prop up the patriarchy.[1] Although this point of view is understandably appealing to women seeking to redefine Christianity and to radicals who intend to reinvent monotheism forever, even women who have never heard of Mary Daly harbor an underlying suspicion that traditional religion has lied to them and that their brothers and fathers just don't get it. Spiritually restless women sense that something about who God is has been withheld from them. They sense a lie being told about the implications of their female bodies on their spiritual lives.

In this search for answers to my spiritual life as a woman, I had to admit that the gender practices of a community say something profound about what that community believes about God. Practice is, after all, theology; we live as we believe. What I saw and heard was not reassuring. I became aware that many in my religious community believed that if God was not literally male, God was at least masculine; therefore, men were better suited to speaking authoritatively about God. In some traditional corners of Christianity, this belief came along with a fear of adding feminine connotations to God—a slippery slope that would lead to calling God "Mother." I could hear the lament over the feminization of the church, which I found odd. Hasn't the church always been referred to as the "bride of Christ"? Of course, what is meant by the feminization of the church is that women are taking over. In this scenario, some women have come to believe that to break the hold that this lie has on us requires that we embrace the feminine face of God and write a new story. It was hard for me, at this point, to blame women for taking this route.

The Feminine Wound

Sue Monk Kidd's poignant *Dance of the Dissident Daughter* tells of her journey from the Christian tradition to the feminine Divine. For women who would otherwise find goddess language off-putting, Kidd makes the feminine Divine particularly relevant. Kidd looks just like us. I could identify with her as she faced her "feminine wound," defined as the "original sin of being born female," and her struggle to wake up from a deep sleep that kept her in a state of spiritual unconsciousness.[2] Kidd says that this struggle to find her voice as a woman was a process of giving birth to herself. I could relate to her increasing awareness that her feminine voice had been muffled. When I read her story, I felt as though I were reading my own.

Still, I was looking not so much to give birth to myself as to hold on to my faith in Jesus, which felt more vital to my self-identity. As I compared notes with Kidd, at times I felt that I was drowning, unable to commit to her conclusions; yet at other times, I was thrilled with new insight. We had asked many of the same questions, gone to the same sources for answers, and come to different conclusions. The struggle to find a unique feminine spirituality wasn't all black and white. There were increasing shades of gray that I would have to negotiate. Like Kidd, I did not want to live the life of a "sanitized" woman—a "good" woman who can't speak from her own knowing. Unlike Kidd, I wasn't ready to ignore Jesus and abandon his historical significance. I came to realize that I could own my faith as a woman, and Jesus would go with me. Plowing through this new territory just meant going the long way around.

Kidd is one example of many women who are caught in this struggle—a very eloquent example. I have gone out of my way to meet women who have left the Christian tradition for one they believe is more woman-friendly. I thought they could help illuminate my own path. More often than not, though, these women had experienced God as a distant, harsh patriarch who has no use for a woman; they, in turn, had no use for a God like that. Others attempted to hold on to Christian tradition by reaching outside the tradition and constructing a hodgepodge of beliefs they could live with. Some women had left the faith and attempted reentry at various points in their lives, only to find themselves put off by the male authority they found within church doors. Others simply felt that Christianity didn't really speak to where they were.

As women are exposed to increased gender awareness in the culture, more of them feel they need to justify staying in any religious tradition. The question becomes no longer whether a spiritually anxious woman will grapple with religious language and symbols, but when. She may do it in secret, but, eventually, she will ask herself the hard questions about God and her feminine life. That questioning can happen at twenty or fifty. When will she attempt to change the words in the hymns from "God of our Fathers" to "God of our Mothers," whispering the changes to herself? When will she be tempted to change the pronouns in the creeds, abolishing the reign of the Father, Son, and Holy Spirit for the Father, Mother, and Child? When, to relieve spiritual hunger, will she weave a new feminist spirituality altogether?

Other women are bringing a distinct gender awareness with them when they enter Christianity. In 2002, when Jane Fonda, a lifelong agnostic, declared on *The Oprah Winfrey Show* that she had embraced Christianity, the media buzzed about her conversion from a previously secular life to being "born again." Many speculated about what this meant for Christianity and for Fonda. I feared that she would soon be confessing her sins on the speaker's circuit. At that time I remember telling several of my friends that I wondered how long she would last before she ran into religious patriarchy. Fonda didn't seem to me like the kind of woman who would put up with blatant sexism. By 2005 Fonda had revealed in her memoir, *My Life So Far,* what happened after her surprise conversion: "It wasn't long, however, before I found myself bumping up against certain literal, patriarchal aspects of Christian orthodoxy that I found difficult to embrace."[3] It was probably inevitable that Fonda would seek out an alternative understanding of Christianity.

Fonda entered into Christianity asking questions that had never even crossed our foremothers' minds. After all, the traditions and roles had remained the same for centuries—men and women doing what had been properly assigned to them.

Men did theology, ran the religious institutions, and kept guard over the faith. Women taught the children, passed along the faith at the kitchen table, and attended to the social needs of the community. For many Christian, Jewish, and even Islamic women, this is no longer enough. We want to "do" religion for ourselves by defining our faith in ways that resonate with our experience. For women and men who are perfectly content in their traditional roles, this questioning feels like a threat to their understanding of God and the divine order of the world. As more and more women have attempted to shape the language and symbols of spirituality, what was once simple and uncomplicated has become a truly messy process.

A Spiritual Boomerang

I grew up in the sixties and seventies when women were experiencing fundamental changes in every area of their lives. Liberal feminism left no part of cultural life untouched. The changes that women sought were largely secular, such as opening career and educational opportunities and securing economic and political advancement. Throughout this period of an energized feminist movement, female groundbreaking events were a constant theme. Women who didn't identify themselves as feminist were benefiting as well from the changes at colleges and in the workplace. The feminist movement was less successful, however, in its attempt to redo our domestic lives by reinventing marriage and redefining motherhood. In part, this was because women themselves would accept only so much change. The changes were substantial enough, though, that educated women were less willing than before to accept what was simply assigned to them.

My peers expected not only to work but also to achieve a lot more through their work. Younger women were told they could do anything, and they grew up expecting that they could control their lives—even their spiritual lives.

During this secular phase, feminism didn't seem to have much use for religion. Many of my friends who were pursuing the new career opportunities might still have gone through the motions of minimal religious participation as they ventured into a church for Christmas or a wedding. What I saw among my peers of professional women was that religion, particularly traditional Christianity, had become irrelevant. Some women lived with a sacred-secular split, which allowed them to be one kind of woman at church and another at work. For a few, feminism became the new religion, but for more and more educated and ambitious women, religion receded to the margins of their lives.

In this new and different world, the old religious language and symbols didn't seem to deliver what many women needed. Religion wouldn't ensure the next promotion at work, and it wouldn't secure political power. It couldn't even get men to do the laundry. More women began to view the purpose of religious institutions as simply to prop up the status quo—keeping men and women in their properly defined place, backed up by the authority of God. Yes, there were always those sentimental souls who had time for religion, but up-and-coming women were busy securing real power.

Then by the early 1990s, the feminist dream ran out of steam, and things began to change again. Women who had found hope in the promise of feminism ran into the feminine difference. We realized that we could work like men, but we ended up with different consequences. We could climb the corporate ladder until a pregnancy threatened to put us on the mommy track. Having tasted enough worldly success to know what it felt like, we finally understood that many of our issues, such as our sense of our own authority, would not be resolved with legal or political power. We were running into walls we never knew existed because we had never gotten this far. We had never stopped to consider that we might be our own obstacle to success.

My peers realized that secular power is a self-limiting process that can only take us so far. After the dust settled from all the changes, interest in religion and spirituality, which historically played a significant role for women, began to return. Yet a traditional religious system seemed to be out of sync with the new realities of self-determined women. Younger women went knocking on church doors, assuming that things had changed, but they were disappointed. The way we practiced religion had not changed. It needed to change.

During the years of transition, not all women abandoned religion. I remained in the church while pursuing new op-portunities in the workplace and somehow navigated the tension that drove other women away. I must admit, though, I was often more comfortable at work than in the American church. Like other major institutions, churches could no longer take women for granted. Women in churches became more interested in studying the women of the Bible. Women had an impact on the religious landscape by entering seminary in record numbers. Feminist theologians scoured the attic of our religious traditions, uncovering family secrets and finding new uses for old ideas. Beliefs that before had been deeply held were no longer sacrosanct and became open to new interpretations more appropriate for the new woman.

The bolder women, to the distress of many, took on the religious hierarchy and were ordained as pastors, priests, and rabbis. They would be there for the many women who eventually sought a cure for their spiritual homelessness.

A FEMINIST THIRST

The time to find a spiritual home had arrived. For me it was like a spiritual spring-cleaning, followed by a garage sale to get rid of what no longer worked. Spirituality writer Carol Flinders sees contemporary women as reconciling a spiritual hunger with a feminist thirst. Many women are now more open to a feminine expression of the Divine that fit their new sensibilities and are asking questions relevant to their spiritual search: What does freedom mean when you are a mother? How do I use my voice effectively in the world when I finally do find it? How do I finally feel at peace with my female body? Many are ready for a new spiritual vocabulary, a new language to articulate our new definition of and relationship to power. The feminine Divine appears to be, if not the answer, at least a way to talk about women's experience.

The latent need that women feel for a woman-affirming spirituality is illustrated by the success of Dan Brown's 2003 bestseller *The Da Vinci Code*. The novel retells Christian history, giving the feminine Divine a prominent place in the plot. Mary Magdalene, who is briefly mentioned in the gospels, becomes the wife of Jesus and bears his love child. Even before this novel made her the heroine *du jour*, Mary Magdalene was a symbol of lost female consciousness over the last two thousand years and is celebrated on her own feast day in Catholic, Episcopal, and Orthodox churches. Brown simply capitalized on what had been there all along.

The Da Vinci Code created a cottage industry of op-ed pieces, commentaries, and online conversations. With cover stories in *Time* and *Newsweek*, and numerous books countering many of the "facts" on which the book is based, it got everybody's attention. Art and church historians weighed in on the obvious factual errors in the book. Whenever I served on panels relating to the women's issues raised by the book, what struck me was not that people would ask questions about church history or how the Bible was written and compiled, but that so many people, particularly women, responded deeply to the theme of the feminine Divine. The book has been so popular among women that one newspaper called it a "craze"—an apt description for how women are viewed when it comes to religion. Women in churches, book clubs, and offices found themselves intrigued with the idea that the feminine Divine has somehow been suppressed by a centuries-long conspiracy. Even young women working for the Feminist Majority—a bastion of political feminism—were excited that the book highlighted the feminine Divine. Never mind that the power of the feminine in Brown's book is a derived power, reduced to sexuality and procreation. They call this progress? Even religiously conservative women found the idea, if not acceptable, at least mischievously appealing. Catholics summoned Mary, Mother of God, as their answer to the issue. The strong feelings evoked by the idea of a church conspiracy to suppress the feminine show women's longing to connect a feminine face or voice with Christianity.[4]

No Religion for Women

Increasingly, women inside and outside the church find that when it comes to God, our female perspective matters after all. Women are seeking and finding something different in the Divine, whether it is within the tradition or outside it. Since theologian Mary Daly's declaration that a religion with a male God was no religion for women, women who are spiritually adventuresome are not just turning to Mary Magdalene or Mary, the mother of Jesus, for models of feminine divinity. Many women have been busy exploring what an altogether alternative spirituality for women would look like.

At a national conference, I attended a workshop on advancing the idea of "the Goddess." I asked, "Does the Goddess serve women well? Do we need this? Does it work?" The resounding answer was "Yes, of course we need her! The Goddess will help women be valued. The Goddess will recapture what has been suppressed about women." Was this true? I had to know.

Interest in the Goddess has been picking up steam in recent years. Like any religion that intends to take up permanent residence as a tradition, it needs a history to give it cultural weight. The legitimacy of the Goddess is currently being put forward by a romanticized myth of a matriarchal prehistory, when women ruled the world and were revered for their life-giving power—a myth that secular leader Gloria Steinem was propagating as early as 1972.[5] I have heard highly educated women bemoan the loss of the ancient matriarchy—an idyllic, harmonious society. The overthrow of this peaceful civilization by patriarchal hordes resulted in hierarchy, violence, and alienation from the earth, which we experience to this day. In *The Myth of Matriarchal Prehistory*, religion scholar Cynthia Eller examines the evidence (or lack thereof) and concludes that there is little archeological basis for believing in an ancient woman-ruled society that worshiped the Goddess. Instead of helping women, the myth of a timeless age of female benevolent rule works to maintain stereotypical ideas about women and men. For many contemporary women it does not matter whether the golden age of matriarchy is a myth or history. What matters is how holding fast to this idea functions in our life. The Goddess has returned with a vengeance to play an important role for many women, causing the whole culture to reevaluate how we view the Divine.

What started as the outgrowth of feminist consciousness-raising groups of the 1960s and 1970s has become the underlying spirituality in women's culture, with the symbol and language of the Goddess now the code for the power and authority of women. Many women no longer believe that they must accept things as they are. We have proven that we can change things by charting a new course and creating new, more empowering stories. Feminist theologian Carol Christ believes that rejecting a male-defined God is not sufficient.[6] God must be replaced with a symbol that evokes the desire in women to see themselves as powerful, deeply connected, and knowing beings. The goddess is everywoman, and everywoman is the goddess—a creative and independent power. As a powerful new metaphor, the goddess influences how women see themselves and their relationship to the Divine.

The feminine Divine is one answer women give to their spiritual questions. For the most part, men led Western theological development by asking questions that were consistent with their experience. Their conclusions reflected the reality that an individual understanding of God is located within a specific individual history and a particular community.[7] Because their curiosity was informed by their own experience, men asked certain questions and ignored others.

Influenced by the Enlightenment, Christian theology began to acquire a need for certainty and began to look and sound much like the science practiced by men.[8] In the name of "universal man," women and their particular perspectives were left out.

"Malestream" theology has emphasized God's attributes of transcendence, justice, power, and dominion, while exhibiting a tendency to silence attributes *culturally* associated with women. Women today who are on a spiritual search for their own knowing have found ways to excavate those previously disregarded attributes of the divine nature, like compassion, nurturance, creativity, and life-giving power—feminine-defined attributes that, when marginalized, result in a dispassionate, unmovable God distant from our everyday lives.

The search for the Goddess assumes that gendered attributes are in opposition to each other, a sort of yin and yang, with women as incurable romantics and men as logical conquerors. According to this way of thinking, in order to embrace the aspects of God that have long been neglected (the cultural feminine), we may have to silence other aspects that are essential to a full understanding of God. Under the surface, however, the search for the feminine Divine assumes that God has a masculine face. We have already accepted what many of us have been given—the masculinization of a God who, in reality, is beyond gender categories. We have forgotten that "feminine" and "masculine" are bodily and socially based categories that can never define the infinite. If we knew a God who was *neither* male nor female but encompassed *all* that is good, we would not settle for either a masculinized God or a Goddess.

In their search for a Divine Being with a different kind of nature, Goddess devotees are not settling for a transcendent Goddess "out there." There is no need for proof that she exists. That would be too similar to the distant God some of us have inherited in our religious legacies. We don't want an abstraction disconnected from our everyday lives. Maybe some women leap into the arms of the Goddess because all of us desperately want the Divine to walk in our Mary Janes. We want a divine being that is near to us and our female experience. Since a hermaphroditic God is just a little hard for anyone to visualize, some women are creating a Westernized, postmodern pantheon offering Greek, African, and Hindu goddesses for our choosing. No matter her name, this new goddess promises to soothe our shaking self-doubt.

Femininity and masculinity, always socially negotiated, were hardwired in the ancient gods and goddesses. Although empowering in one sense, this is limiting in another. Whether benevolent or malevolent, the Goddess embodies the best and the worst of what we believe about woman's nature. As creators of symbols, we project onto the Divine our highest human aspirations: love, courage, creativity, and a profound sense of justice and beauty. The great and "good" Mother is the domestic weaver—a powerful intuitive, waiting for our call.

We also project onto the Divine our greatest fears and the worst of our humanity. On a bad PMS day, the Goddess is the bitch, the woman scorned, the undomesticated wild and dangerous one. In the ancient pantheon, all the devotion, treachery, and jealousy of human relationships were played out in the commotion of divine life. Kali-Ma, the Hindu goddess of death and rebirth, becomes the Dark Mother who chews up and swallows her own baby.

Pop culture also reflects women's spiritual wanderings into the realm of the Goddess. Even though serious devotees of Goddess religion seek to emphasize the interdependence of all life, popular notions of the Goddess are highly individualistic. In the pop version of goddess spirituality, we read *The Red Tent*, take Web quizzes to discover the goddess who fits us best, and incorporate her into our vocabulary. Goddess religion has never been monotheistic, so there is a goddess for every need. We can call on an inner goddess who understands our motivations and will nurture us into becoming the women we were meant to be. Lilith is the original rambunctious feminist, meeting our need to assert ourselves. We can call on Ishtar for fertility, Tara for compassion, or, closer to home, the Virgin of Guadalupe for liberation. Of course, there is Aphrodite, goddess of love, Athena, goddess of wisdom, and the Martha Stewart of goddesses, Hestia, goddess of the hearth, through whom we can recapture cozy domesticity by erecting home altars out of the mementos of our lives. We can purchase herbal teas, aromatherapy soaps, and fashion to fit the feminine Divine within ourselves. In fact, the goddess has become so integrated with consumerism, I expect I'll soon catch her shopping at Banana Republic!

As good as this sounds, the current benevolent and romanticized symbol of the Goddess is not an accurate one; the goddess that is now emerging seems cut off from her real history. According to Near East scholar Tikva Frymer-Kensky, the ancient goddesses were not enshrined for the benefit of women but were one aspect of the official religion of male-dominated societies.[9] In pagan cultures, where female infanticide was completely accepted and abortion was frequently imposed on women, the goddess cult remained mysteriously silent. Could it be that the idea of Goddess was part of patriarchy's underpinning? Goddess worship never resulted in equality for women.

In ancient religions, a deity's gender was crucial to the role and function he or she played within a polytheistic system. More often than not, the goddess's divine power was tied to her biological role as mother. Because the goddess was associated with fertility, she often required bloody and terrifying appeasement if earth and womb were to yield their fruit. The Goddess ensconced motherhood forever into the sacred and cosmic realm, solidifying real women's "feminine" (read "frail and disempowered") place in the world. Do we want the Divine to be subject to our limits, our foibles, and our oppressions? Perhaps in the desire to have our voices heard and our experience acknowledged, we have created a Divine saddled with our troubles, often finding themselves paramours, sorrowful mothers, and rape victims of male counterparts. Did they fare any better than the rest of us? In goddess spirituality, instead of freedom to become what we wish, we may be setting ourselves up to become merely victims of a philandering Zeus.

Nevertheless, the popular goddesses of today are fun and sexy symbols of where women are now, speaking for women and identifying with our contemporary experience. As I sought to find answers to my own questions about God, however, I found the goddess to be too familiar for my spiritual comfort. As revealed by book titles such as *A Goddess Is a Girl's Best Friend*, she is too chummy, too hip to produce a sense of awe. I saw that as we attempt to validate our experiences, we risk being trapped by them. The popular goddesses of today seem to confirm what culture has believed all along: women are spirituality trite and inconsequential.

I learned other important things on my tour through goddess spirituality. Women's collective impulse toward the goddess yields some positive results, in that it requires that we get beyond making God an abstraction. Our view of the Divine must be connected to our real lives in some way. I learned that the appeal of the Goddess grows out of women's quest for freedom to become a whole human being with the capacity *both* to nurture *and* effect change in the world. We want to speak from our own female knowing, yet at the same time, many of us are uncomfortable with the implications wrapped up in the Goddess. We want a spirituality that can accommodate the individual particulars of each seeker—gender, race, and social placement—without reducing us to those particulars. We want to build a flourishing community that also includes men. I came to see that our view of God had to be fuller and richer in order for women to finally feel as though they could come home.

With all this mix of positive and negative possibilities, what purpose does the feminine Divine serve, not only for women but for society as a whole? The search for the feminine face of the Divine is an attempt to correct a distortion about God's nature and about women's reflections of God's image. The emergence of the feminine Divine has filled a cultural need in our search for holistic knowledge and spirituality because our religious ideas are affected by cultural values and biases. In a society where science and technology are the main modes of success (and, therefore, being), men are associated with progress, rationality, and conquest of nature, and women are associated with the body and nature; the feminine has been devalued. This knowledge split, combined with the social power that men hold, has ultimately resulted in the masculinization of God, who becomes a symbol of order and control and whose name is invoked in order to keep women in line. As women have gained social power, they themselves have attempted to project onto God their own experience and understanding of the world. (The divine oneness continues to be made into our human projection of a dualistic world.) The result is a battle between a feminine and masculine deity and a struggle to determine which one is worthy of women's allegiance.

The reemergence of the Goddess as a woman and nature-affirming deity signals a search for a spirituality that is close to where we live: in our bodies and the natural world. Even as technology and media privilege one kind of knowledge through goddess spirituality, women are asserting a different kind of knowledge claim that has been identified with them all along: an intuitive and interconnected way of knowing. The feminine Divine appears to be a ready-made metaphor for the knowledge the current culture devalues. Very much like the Romantic poets' response to the Enlightenment, Starhawk, a leading voice for earth-based and goddess religion, expresses and responds to the current estrangement many women feel. Instead of a radically individualistic, alienated way of being, she seeks the spiritual consciousness of "immanence—the awareness of the world and everything in it as alive, dynamic, interdependent, interacting, and infused with moving energies: a living being, a weaving dance."[10] For many of us who crave community, affirmation of our bodies, and reconnection to the earth, Starhawk's notion of immanence answers many questions. The fleshiness we crave in our religious experiences gets lost in traditional theological abstractions. Devotion to the Goddess attempts to bridge that gulf.

The goddess symbol embraces women as life givers from first menstruation to menopause. Instead of evoking deep shame, the rhythms and cycles of women's lives are seen as powerful events; by creating rituals for first menstruation and menopause, women are taking these significant milestones out of the dark. In a time when we are increasingly alienated from our bodies through a variety of body-assaulting means, from abortion to cosmetic surgery, we long for a spirituality that recognizes our powerful bodily experiences. As we struggle to overcome self-doubt and become holders of wisdom, the goddess allows women to frame questions for the culture. Can women be authentic knowers, in both an intuitive and an intellectual sense, and actors in the world instead of tentative participants? Can women know the Divine for themselves? Can women gain the authority to speak and act out that knowledge? In order to answer these questions, women are attempting to create out of new cloth a feminist spirituality that puts us at the center of the knowing process. My fear, however, is that embracing the Goddess in this way deprives us of the possibility of a holistic, woman-affirming spirituality within the Jesus tradition. For me, such deprivation is not a viable option.

Jesus or Sophia?

As I wrestled with my questions about God, I wondered: Would the Jesus tradition allow me to answer the questions I was asking? I couldn't affirm tradition for tradition's sake. Our religious experience could no longer be about simply repeating what has been handed to us, no questions asked. To be responsible spiritual beings requires that we question what we are given so we can come to own it for ourselves. Yet unlike professional feminist theologians, I didn't have the luxury of speculating by deconstructing everything I had inherited. Neither was I ready to throw out the baby with the bath water. I had experienced the essential core of the Christian faith as true, even though I found certain cultural expressions of it perplexing. I also had to make this work in real life, which for me meant staying connected to my roots. My need to reconcile women's contemporary experience with my faith took me back to my childhood.

I first learned about Jesus on the streets and in the plazas of my native Buenos Aires—literally, on the streets; my early childhood was not spent in church buildings. Church was a semiformal community of believers who gathered together on Friday night for three hours of prayer and singing in preparation to go out on Saturday and Sunday and proclaim the good news. Sunday school consisted of Bible stories illustrated with flannel-board figures put up in the narrow alleys of *villas miserias,* the desperately poor shantytowns into which we ventured. I learned about Jesus by listening and doing. I learned about Jesus by seeing hopelessly marginal people emerge from alcoholism, lifelong unemployment, and domestic abuse. The combination of a radical faith and an empowering community made this life transformation possible.

This living, breathing spirituality was embodied in an active faith with an overarching concern for justice for the worker, the poor, and the less powerful and was driven by a belief in the pursuit of justice on earth and the faith that a new community would eventually be ushered in. Our Protestant community saw itself as outside the dominant religious and social system. Our community was by no means perfect, but it did provide me with glimpses of what was possible. As a Protestant in a Catholic country, I gained an institutional outsider's sensitivity. This "outsider" view has shaped my Christianity and now serves me well in understanding my female spiritual experience. In fact, the treasure trove of wisdom in this living tradition allowed me to begin making the connection between the wisdom of Jesus and the wisdom women are seeking today.

My encounter with women who were using the name Sophia as a divine name pushed me to look at Jesus in a different way. Had Jesus and Sophia emerged out of the same tradition? The Jewish culture in which Jesus lived was steeped in the wisdom tradition of the Hebrew sages. It embraced an essential idea about the nature of God: Yahweh is One. This God of Israel was the eternally wise Creator who abolished the entire complex pantheon known at the time. Yahweh had been revealed to Moses as the "I AM WHO I AM"—a self-defined being who was absolute in perfection, power, and beauty. God was not only a consuming fire of justice but also of love, expressing compassion and mercy toward his people. Today, we take for granted the statement that God is love, but in the ancient polytheistic system, gods weren't concerned with love for humanity. The establishment of Yahweh as an all-encompassing God was a major break from the surrounding polytheistic culture, setting Israel apart as God's covenant people.

Even though the sages understood God's loving-kindness and mercy, they also believed that Yahweh could never be known directly. To break into the pure, divine presence meant certain death. God bridged this gulf by saying, "I am coming to you in the thickness of a cloud."[11] The cloud—God's hiddenness—allowed them the possibility of insight into the mystery of Divine Wisdom, protecting his people and awakening awe in them.[12] Israel gained a veiled glimpse into Divine Wisdom.

Jewish scriptures reveal God's power as his creative Word, which shapes reality and brings life out of nothingness. God's Word, once uttered, has a life of its own. God's Word is not merely a collection of sounds or of letters on a page; the Word is an independent reality. The Jewish people understood that without the Word, there is no wisdom, and by God's Word, we receive the Wisdom of God: "For the Lord giveth wisdom: and out of his mouth cometh understanding."[13] The ordinary person only heard God's Word through priest or prophet, never directly. God also made himself known through miraculous historical events like fire from heaven, a parting of the sea, and earthquakes. Prophets had to interpret these infrequent events, which meant that on a day-to-day basis, the ordinary person was on her own, left to follow a complex religious code and wait for a coming Messiah.

Against this backdrop, the Jewish sages sought to give common people guidance for everyday life, to make sense of the mundane, and to read the world for the wisdom of God that is revealed in it. By studying nature and humanity, they tried to give people a "God of the gaps"—one infused in daily life. Because they believed God created everything through the power of his Word, God's Wisdom permeated everything. The sages sought to decipher and teach the wisdom that was hidden from the casual observer. The rich, deep tradition infuses their wisdom literature, which offers guidance on work, family life, civic culture, sexuality, and fair dealings in the marketplace; they even provided counsel on how to make and keep friends, choose a spouse, rear a child, and order one's life to yield abundance and longevity. For thousands of years, the questions they asked and attempted to answer have remained relevant and still interest us today. While growing up I was encouraged to read the wisdom literature, which, more often than not, was puzzling. But I did gain a sense that there was rhyme and reason to life, an inherent but hidden wise poetry to our days.

One of the most remarkable features of the wisdom literature is the sages' description of wisdom as a woman. In the *Meshalin*, or biblical Proverbs, Woman Wisdom is identified with God, present at Creation and infusing all. She seeks close engagement with the world and delights to be with humanity. Contrary to gender-stereotyped images of women, she is in no way passive but is portrayed as a liberator and an establisher of justice, a lover in pursuit of humanity who, in return, responds to those who love her.

Woman Wisdom is a strong literary tool with no equal in the biblical literature. Woman Wisdom is more than a simple personification but is not quite a personal being. Theological speculation about why the Jewish sages attempted to speak about wisdom with a feminine metaphor has yielded different interpretations. Is Woman Wisdom strictly a one-dimensional personification of an attribute of God? Is Woman Wisdom a sneaky disguise for the Goddess? Or is she simply a tool of a patriarchal system with no redeeming role for real women? One possible answer is that she reflects the influence of women sages in the royal courts. Another is that the literature's emphasis on knowledge gained through daily life is highly associated with women. Regardless, I believe Woman Wisdom can be, for us, a positive model of female power.

One of the key aspects is Woman Wisdom's strength and possession of her own knowing. Woman Wisdom preaches with authority, orders the world through her creative agency, and welcomes all to her table.[14] Woman Wisdom is eager to teach us the way to long life, justice, and abundance. In the streets, she cries out to those who need direction. Over the noise of the marketplace, she promises to protect those who follow her and laughs at those who don't listen. There is no hesitation in her voice, no doubt in her proclamation. She demands attention, and there is nothing timid about her. It's a rare woman who will dare speak with her level of confidence.

Woman Wisdom also has a nemesis—the Woman of Folly—who leads foolish young men astray into chaos and confusion. Instead of life, she offers death to those who follow her. Both seductive and dangerous, Woman of Folly borrows from a negative view of women. Yet the intent of these literary devices is not to teach about good and bad women; rather, it illustrates two ways of life. The way of Woman Wisdom offers abundance and life. We are advised to follow in her way.

The role and meaning of Woman Wisdom is best understood in the context of an ancient culture. Monotheistic Israel was surrounded by cultures in which numerous household gods and goddesses were the norm, any of which could be called on for help with household, field, and livestock. All members of a household had their own personal god to help them fulfill their designated role. Today, goddess figurines have become trendy, fun things to have around for décor and a bit of inspiration, but for ancient people, these gods were crucial to their view of the world. This pantheon provided a sense of order in a frightening world.[15] Imagine how isolated from their neighbors an ordinary Jewish family felt. Yahweh was such an overarching deity that they were forbidden to reduce God to a mere stone figure. The lack of a physical symbol for God denied the Jewish people the emotional comfort they must have seen in the household idols of their neighbors. Sometimes the temptation was too great, so they joined their neighbors and worshiped the same gods.

Through Woman Wisdom, the Jewish sages could provide their people with a picture of the immanence of God.[16] Without compromising God's oneness and transcendence, they could borrow from the surrounding cultures' understanding of divinity as closely related to wisdom.[17] In response to the surrounding religions that worshiped the earth and tried to appease its wrathful nature, they could embrace their own theology of Creation by which they placed all created things under the Creator.[18] Therefore, instead of fearing the natural world, people could be comforted by the wisdom of the earth, our sister. Over time this understanding of wisdom grew in complexity for the Jewish people, finally becoming associated with Torah—God's commandments and covenant with his people.[19]

Out of this rich Hebrew understanding of wisdom came Jesus, preaching in the tradition of Woman Wisdom. From a young age, he is described as filled with wisdom. Jesus calls on those who are marginalized and lost to come to him. Speaking in parables, paradoxical sayings, and indirect figurative language, all of which is characteristic of wisdom literature, he left many to wonder what he meant. Jesus, the sage, delivered one-liners like, "Follow me, and let the dead bury the dead" or "If the blind lead the blind, both will fall into a ditch"—sayings that often puzzled his closest disciples. His parables were short stories that invited the listener to see things from a different point of view. Through parables he created a world of reversals where the first was last and the last first, where the worldly wise became fools and insiders found themselves shut out. With repetitive themes of justice and wisdom, Jesus continually directed his listeners to the ancient Jewish scriptures as a source of understanding.

When asked by his closest followers why he spoke in parables instead of speaking plainly, he said, "Because it has been given to you to know the mysteries of the kingdom of heaven, but to them it has not been given."[20] Like Woman Wisdom, Jesus presented himself as holding hidden wisdom that only he could reveal. Like the ancient sages, he made an otherwise inaccessible God available to the ordinary person. In this way, Jesus reclaimed the wisdom tradition from those who had reduced it to obedience to the law. Knowing God would be reflected in embodied wisdom rather than knowledge of the law and religious observance. The everyday practices in one's life, such as actively loving one's neighbor, were how a true relationship with God would be measured. The followers of Jesus, shaped by the Jewish sage tradition, recognized the wisdom nature of his teaching.

Jesus didn't hesitate to claim the authority of Woman Wisdom. Presenting himself as Wisdom, he said, "Someone greater than Solomon is here"—a remarkable claim to the ears of people who considered Solomon the greatest sage of all. Opposed by the religious power brokers, he declared that the Queen of Sheba, who had sought out the wisdom of Solomon, would stand in judgment of them. By implication, a woman was wiser than they—an obvious insult within a patriarchal system. In defending his healing work to those who opposed him, he simply said, "Wisdom is justified by her deeds."[21] In rebuking those who burden people with religious rules, he responded, "Therefore the Wisdom of God also said. . . ."[22] In his teaching and action, Jesus claimed the Wisdom of God as his own identity. Jesus took the wisdom tradition of the Jewish sages a step further. He dispensed with speaking for God but instead spoke as the Wisdom of God— a declaration that enraged the religious authorities and moved others to faith.[23] Those who believed him had good reason to come to the conclusion that Jesus *himself* was the embodiment of Wisdom and not just one of the many traveling sages of the time. In one parable with a striking similarity to what is found in the wisdom literature, Jesus tells of a woman who is seeking a lost coin. Quickly she lights a lamp and thoroughly sweeps her house. When she finds the coin, she calls her friends to celebrate with her, because what was lost is now found.[24] Those who heard this simple parable would have recognized the search for Wisdom and Wisdom searching for those who are lost. When Jesus said that he had come to seek that which was lost, by implication he was identifying himself as Wisdom looking for lost humanity. His audience was baffled.

Jesus' claims to both divinity and wisdom left no room for opposition. He spoke in the first person in what are known as the "I AM" sayings. In a series of public addresses, Jesus identified himself by saying, I am the bread of life, I am the light of the world, I am the door, I am the life, and I am the authentic wine. These statements echoed God's self-disclosure to Moses; his audience would recognize them as images from wisdom literature.[25] Woman Wisdom had made the same claims. The parallelism between Woman Wisdom and Jesus is striking. Repeatedly through his teachings, Jesus declared himself not only to be Wisdom among us but also God.

The wisdom tradition was such an essential part of the Jewish understanding of God that early Christians began to talk about Jesus as the Wisdom of God. Early hymns and songs reflect the understanding of Wisdom as the Word—the logos of God—made flesh. As Christians reread the Jewish scripture, they heard in Woman Wisdom the voice of Jesus, the Christ. In their understanding there was no way to separate wisdom, by which the world was created, from the breathing, living Jesus who walked their dusty roads. Wisdom cloaked in human flesh is neither inaccessible nor disconnected from our history; rather, it's acquainted with our ways: hunger, pain, suffering, weariness, and, ultimately, death. In Jesus, his early followers experienced Wisdom as a healing, creating, and celebratory power attuned to their bodies and the earth.

Like the ancient Jewish people, we feel that the God we inherited has become inaccessible to us, not only as women but as human beings. God seems too distant from our everyday pain and pleasure. We are left unable to read our lives, understand their underlying meaning, or make sense of our inconsistencies. We need a recovery of the wisdom tradition of the Jewish sages and of Jesus—a tradition that teaches us to seek wisdom through the observation of nature, attention to sacred text, and a community that shares in a common history. Ultimately, this tradition teaches that the path to true wisdom is through an encounter with the eternally wise God. I believe we can recover the wisdom we need. Even as Woman Wisdom speaks with authority, it is our encounter with the Wisdom of God that will allow us the power to know and speak for ourselves. It will break through our self-doubt and allow us to flourish as women in the world. As wisdom seekers we experience multiple barriers, some that we built and others that have been built for us. In the next chapters we will look at some of the barriers that have kept women from experiencing this type of knowledge of God and of ourselves.

Wisdom calls aloud in the streets, she raises her voice in the public squares; she calls out at the street corners, she delivers her message at the city gates.

Proverbs 1:20–21

2

THE INTUITIVE EDGE

As an eight-year-old Spanish-speaking immigrant from Argentina, I learned that language and culture are inseparably linked. Words can never tell all; their meaning arises out of a nuanced and lived experience in a particular community. In the United States of the mid-sixties, I not only had to learn how to manipulate my tongue in new ways; I also had to acquire a taste for Dr. Pepper, learn the significance of a Thanksgiving turkey, and figure out why Donna Reed wore pearls while vacuuming. I did this by hearing and coming to understand the American story.

Once I could name the many new experiences I was encountering, I began to feel more like I belonged—but not entirely. I felt a sense of inadequacy in trying to interpret this new world for my parents, and I quickly learned that many important things get lost in translation. Many things that "speak American" did not have an Argentinean equivalent and vice versa. As a small girl my favorite flavor was *dulce de leche*; it wasn't peanut butter or chocolate. But trying to explain this in English was unsatisfying; caramel only approximates it. There is more to *dulce de leche* than milk and sugar cooked to a burnt color. It is a whole way of being—an attitude about food, community, and special occasions.

At the same time there were things I knew about the world that seemed strange to my new neighbors but were part of my self-definition, like the experience of drinking *mate* around a table, with static-filled tango music blaring from an old radio. My new neighbors didn't know the lively smell of *asado* or how wonderful cold sparkling cider could be on a smoldering hot Christmas Eve. I, however, had never seen or imagined snow until our first cold Christmas in Kansas. And I was used to a new visitor, who might even be unshaven, greeting me with a physical embrace, while my new American friends seldom touched people who were outside their intimate circle. These experiences added to the awareness that these two cultures had different ways of looking at the world.

Memories of Argentina did not serve me well in my attempts to feel included; they made me feel odd and strangely homeless. Desperate for acceptance among my age mates, I had to learn a new language—a new story—and forget or suppress the first. But to forget the mother tongue would be to forget a part of myself. So in order to be true, to live in integrity with a complex identity, I learned to live in two worlds: one was my Argentinean world, and the other was my new American world. We all take on the language of the dominant community as our own and, in a sense, forget our own internal language. Life is a journey to recover this original language and own our knowing. But oddly enough, we can't do this alone; we find the means to make this journey in community.

A woman taking on the language of the community is silenced in particular ways, just as my Americanization silenced my Argentinean experience. Historically, many parts of our experience of the world remained unnamed. They were never written down. Even as *woman* became the scientific subject of study, she did not possess the social power to tell her own story until very recently. Those innumerable stories of women's experience of the world—in all their kaleidoscopic diversity, from motherhood to warrior—have been lost. Consequently, as contemporary women, we find ourselves piecing together fragmented stories of those who have gone before. We have a desperate need to catch up on this lost history. Biographies of twentieth-century women such as Simone Weil, Beryl Markham, and Edna St. Vincent Millay made me aware of parts of my life that had remained unspoken. And because a woman was courageous enough to call sexual harassment what it was, I finally understood that I had been sexually harassed, years after the actual experience. This ability to name experience is provided by the community. When women become equal-speaking participants in a community, previous tacit knowledge that women hold is given a voice. The human story is fuller.

We enter into the history of the community through the stories that language makes possible. Stories about a crazy uncle, the struggles of our grandmother, and our parents' romance help us make sense of who we are. The larger cultural stories, such as Adam and Eve, Snow White, and Joan of Arc, provide reference points for where we belong in the larger human story. The power of stories gives us access to another type of knowledge: knowledge that is outside ourselves. Over time this objective knowledge becomes the authoritative voice, overriding what we access through our own experience.

As we seek community affirmation, we learn early to question our internal stirrings. What if we experience work or family very differently from the stories we have been told? These external stories have the sound of parental authority, the sound of how things should be. Echoed over and over, they ring truer and more real than our own feelings. We begin to question ourselves. In fact, we begin to silence our experiential knowledge, regarding it as illegitimate. This cycle of experience—seeking outside affirmation and silencing our inner knowledge—continues throughout life.

FEMININE POSTURING

Women often display a pervasive lack of confidence in their own experience-based knowledge. It's easy not to trust what we have lived. Some women come right out and say, "Don't listen to me. I don't know anything." This statement startles me, especially when it's coming from a fifty-year-old woman. Often I am not talking to women specifically about this reluctance to claim knowledge. Most of us are savvy enough to understand how completely unfeminist, if not unfashionable, it is to express a lack of confidence. But as I listen to what women say, I hear a consistent refrain of self-doubt: the hand-wringing over decisions, relationships, and work that a good talk over coffee with a friend doesn't seem to alleviate; all those "I don't know" statements and the frequent apologies for the inconsequential that sound like, "I'm sorry I'm taking up space in the world." I notice otherwise smart women constantly second-guessing themselves. We seek reassurance that we are not crazy, that maybe what our gut is telling us is true. This self-doubt, combined with the reluctance to act and speak based on our own knowing, makes us needy for constant reassurance. I am surrounded by accomplished women and incredulous that this need remains a permanent fixture of life for many of them. Nevertheless, contemporary women are plagued by a particular kind of self-doubt, which may be a hazard of being female.

To be unsure of ourselves, to question what we know and how to live pervades all human experience. It's the stuff that makes for good drama: Hamlet's "to be or not to be." It isn't as if men don't experience self-doubt, though. Witness those broody, creative types that some of us find so fascinating. However, in listening to women I notice that something else is going on. Our self-doubt, our hesitation, isn't simply our humanity or our temperament. Many of us have received a particular type of training that views self-assurance in speech and action as the quintessential male position and, therefore, unfeminine. We are more likely than men to couch our words, to hedge our opinions, and to develop a general hesitancy toward action. To do otherwise might make us appear to be pushy or a bitch.

When we find ourselves unable to make the choice between what we know and what we are told to be, the paralysis of self-doubt spills over into every area of our lives. It's easy to be caught between not knowing whether we should follow the financial advice in Tuesday's horoscope or a no-nonsense financial planner. Women who are fabulously successful in one area of their lives can find themselves completely clueless in others. Even mega-star Madonna confessed to worrying about whether she had said the right thing in an interview or if she is taking good enough care of the people in her life.[1] Self-doubt shows up in an inability to speak with assurance or to act in a way that is truly authentic. We can see the pervasiveness of self-doubt in the number of books on why women sabotage their own careers, don't admit their ambitions, or make lousy negotiators. The number of books that address these issues reminds me of the many talented businesswomen I have known who continue to underprice their work. They don't value what they know. This persistent self-doubt often leaves us living tentative lives, waiting for a clarifying event—a new relationship, a job opening, or maybe just a pair of Prada shoes—to tell us who we ought to be.

A consequence of all this unease is that many of us suffer from some form of wobbly thinking—that back-and-forth waffling that is defined by an inability to commit to our own experiential knowing. We remain perpetually open to the demands of whatever surrounds us, resulting in the job with the nightmare boss we stayed in for too long, the boyfriend who continually disappointed us but who we couldn't seem to give up, and the mortgage we talked ourselves into, even though we really didn't want or need one more responsibility. We find ourselves second-guessing our decisions and coming up short.

In pursuing all the new possibilities available to women, we forget to ask these questions: What does my life require? What is it asking of me? These may be the most frightening questions. With more education and information and with more professionals advising us, where does true wisdom emerge? In a postfeminist world, where the equality of the sexes is taken for granted, many are living starkly conventional, womanly lives. On the surface our lives may look different from those of our foremothers, but on a deeper level we are experiencing the same old problems. It seems that the feminist revolution has rearranged the furniture but forgotten to clean out the closet.

With enough space to think, maybe we could find some clarity and feel something fresh, like opening a window in a stuffy room. Maybe all we need is to follow the advice in women's magazines to listen to our own voice, to follow our own inner wisdom. If we could do that, *Real Simple* would be more than another magazine cluttering our already crowded lives; instead, we carry a persistent, nagging sense of inadequacy in the pit of our stomach. This is part of the existential crisis that spirituality writer Starhawk calls "consciousness estrangement" from the world and ourselves. It will take more than therapy or journaling workshops to feel fully connected to our lives. We need a way to access the spiritual selves we've buried under piles of distorted messages about what it means to be a woman and what a woman can know.

ANCIENT WISDOM

The ancient sages' cure for this disconnection from ourselves and the world was the acquisition of wisdom. What did they mean by *wisdom*, and how do we view it now? To the contemporary mind, the idea of wisdom can sound rather mystifying. Becoming wise does not sound particularly attractive or sexy. We want to be rich and in control of our destiny—but wise? Most of us seek to be clever or to acquire a certain amount of market savvy; we are told to trumpet our own "managerial know-how" or "people skills." We don't highlight "being wise" on a résumé as a marketable skill. We have learned to measure people by their hard-earned accomplishments, their IQ, and their fashion sense, never their wisdom. Wisdom sounds so staid. Why would we ever want it?

Our popular understanding of wisdom is drawn for us as we grow up. We hear about "mother's wisdom"—those sayings about clean underwear and the value of eating our carrots. Our wisdom teeth come in, signaling the end to childhood; we meet wise guys, whom we find so annoying. Then we hear about the wisdom of old age, which we certainly want to avoid. In all these understandings, wisdom remains trite—a consolation prize society offers people it deems as not having any real power.

Later in life we learn that wisdom is hard to pin down and even harder to come by. It may be the only good you salvage from a bad relationship: *Never do that again.* Perhaps wisdom is marked by gray hairs, signaling that you have been around the block a few times. Some of us grew up with pop sages like Abigail Van Buren dispensing contemporary wisdom in every morning paper through her column, "Dear Abby." Whether their advice made you cringe or not, Van Buren, along with her sister Ann Landers, always had an answer to some bewildered person's dilemma. The readers got to live vicariously through the blunders of others, as Abby and Ann castigated some and cheered others on, but apparently the folksy wisdom they dispensed to others failed to heal their own lifelong rift. It does seem that wisdom is a hit-or-miss proposition. You may have wise counsel for others but not be able to answer your own questions. You may be wise in one situation and find yourself completely empty-handed in the next. And sometimes those who appear wise can give us bad advice. Wisdom is elusive.

We have come to regard wisdom as something left on the bookshelves of history or some esoteric quality a few special people achieve. We have heard of "the wisdom of the ages" or the nebulous wisdom of the body or the earth, as in Christiane Northrup's *Women's Bodies, Women's Wisdom.* Pop icon Madonna, along with other celebrities, has reclaimed the ancient Kabbalist wisdom tradition as her own. Others explore Buddhist wisdom under the leadership of the popular Dalai Lama, whose title means "ocean of wisdom."

The ancient philosophers and sages had a great deal to say about wisdom. To the Buddha, wisdom, which is distinct from normal intelligence, was one of six practical disciplines that enabled a person to reach Enlightenment. To Sophocles, wisdom was the supreme part of happiness. Cicero saw it as giving us the ability to discriminate between good and evil, between what is best and what is hurtful. The ancient sages were much more comfortable pondering and talking about wisdom than we are today.

The Jewish sages, who borrowed heavily from international wisdom, believed that through careful attention to patterns in the world, one could find a harmonious life. The king of the Jewish sages was Solomon, whose collection of wise sayings included the advice to pursue wisdom above all. Even today, complex and difficult dilemmas are said to require the "wisdom of Solomon" to sort out. Solomon's wisdom embodies the understanding and savvy required to navigate what appears to be a no-win situation.

The Jewish sages understood the acquisition of wisdom to be a three-fold process. First, it was critical to pay attention to nature because of the wisdom inherent in creation. The sages believed wisdom was to be found in the harmony of earth's chaotic and ordered cycles. Second, they considered community to be vital to gaining wisdom, as one generation passed along its experience to another, and parents passed on the culture's stories, proverbs, and sayings to their children to guide them through life. Third, the Jewish sages believed we acquire wisdom through an encounter with the God who breaks into our lives.[2] They considered seeking a divine encounter to be essential to acquiring true wisdom. Wisdom—a deep knowing and connectedness to God—was the greatest wealth a person could possess. Ultimately, for the ancient sages, acquiring wisdom was a spiritual journey.

In ancient wisdom literature, wisdom is often personified as a woman—a fact that has recently caught the attention of many. From the Greeks' Athena to Gnostic Christianity's Sophia, wisdom, in the form of a woman, is the creator and sustainer of life. There is Brigid of the Celtic tradition, whose threefold wisdom in healing, metal work, and poetry is ready to guide us. There is Saraswati, the Hindu goddess of wisdom, without whose presence the world falls into chaos and confusion. Over and over the connection between women and wisdom shows up in the literature of other cultures. Perhaps this stems from the universal understanding that woman is the holder of a particular type of cultural knowledge that is passed on from generation to generation. After all, the mother is the first source of practical, everyday wisdom for young children. As we seek healing for our self-doubt and to live with coherence and meaning, perhaps there is something for us in this diverse and ancient understanding of wisdom.

Our Crisis of Knowing

In the meantime, many contemporary women are seeking wisdom through a recovery of old-fashioned women's intuition. We hope that by returning to this neglected part of woman's knowing, we will be able to heal our self-doubt and gain the spiritual self-assurance we lack. I have noticed that the attempt to access our intuitive selves often shows up in unlikely places—like a women's business conference. More than once I have found myself sitting in a grand ballroom full of well-heeled, yet time-pressed women, waiting to be reminded of our womanly difference—our intuitive advantage. At these women's conferences, I have sat on the edge of my seat listening to over-achieving speakers, Olympic gold medalists, and women with famous fathers instructing me to listen to my inner voice, to embrace my power, and to begin with positive self-talk.

Then comes the moment when I think, "She can't be serious." This is when a speaker leads the whole room in obediently repeating mantras that end with "I am all." Despite their inspiring stories of overcoming obstacles and winning trophies, I draw the line at the affirmations. Not only does this exercise of repeating mantras out loud and out of context make everyone look and feel silly, but I doubt anyone believes them. Rather than soothing my self-doubt, the speaker's performance and our insincere affirmations only underscore our feelings of insignificance, inadvertently leading to the conclusion that the speaker is special and that the gods have smiled on her. Unlike her, I have to be hand-held through self-actualization. I sense that what we have here is an exceptional woman on a really nice trip, and she has found a secret I desperately want in on. While her voice sounds loud and courageous, I am left straining to hear my own whimper.

The mantra of the day is to "follow our inner voice," but the expression is used in so many different ways that it's hard to know what anyone is actually talking about. What exactly is the inner voice? Is it God, is it me, or is it me-as-God? To some the inner voice is the child within that is unfettered with life's baggage. To others it's the authentic self or simply a person's intuition—that feeling or belief in an internal sixth sense; Webster's dictionary defines *intuition* as the "act or process of coming to direct knowledge or certainty without reasoning or inferring: immediate conviction without rational thought."[3] In our daily life we share this intuition with our friends through our insightful advice, a gift from our internal wise sage who just knows our friend is making a dreadful mistake.

Historically, intuition looks very different, depending on who is displaying it. Intuition in men can often pass for inspiration—sometimes divine inspiration at that. In women, intuition looks like we have given in to our "natural" empathetic emotions (or maybe just a bad case of PMS). Whatever it is, intuition has been culturally understood to be part of the feminine world, like cooking and mothering. It has been called women's wisdom (or foolishness) and considered part of her domain. It has been scorned, belittled, and sometimes admired, but mostly considered unreliable. How women and men view it differs significantly and depends to a great extent on our experience.

Our contemporary understanding of intuition has been shaped by therapeutic and spiritual definitions referring to our highest dreams and aspirations. Writers use it to express what they know to be the truth. Anne Lamott calls intuition our "broccoli"—a way to help us distinguish our own voice from the negative voice of our mother that we have internalized.[4] Lamott understands that one of the greatest obstacles to writing and to life is the inability to listen to what we already know is true. This is an internal sense of the truth that more authoritative voices often override. However we define *intuition,* there is evidence that a whole lot of knowing takes place under the radar of reason.

Regardless of whether we know how to listen to our intuition, or even know what it is, we all come to acknowledge it after suffering the consequences of not heeding it too many times. It's also easy to hold a romantic notion of intuition and believe that if we follow this wise inner guide, we can avoid catastrophes and find self-actualization—that is, we'll feel fulfilled as human beings. This belief is part of the notion that under layers of social conditioning we can find a self that acts and speaks with confidence: that self just *knows.* Unfortunately, it's not that simple.

What we want to believe about intuition—its accessibility, its readiness to give us wise answers—is at odds with what we have been taught about what counts as legitimate knowledge. Our attempt to grasp true knowing is frustrated by our inherited attitudes about *what* we can know and *how* we can know. Our cultural paradigm has shaped a hierarchy of knowledge in which intuition is clearly a lower form. Our families, educational institutions, and workplaces continually teach and reinforce this.

The knowledge valued by our culture is rational, scientific, objective, and accessible through detached observation independent of human concerns. Claims about truth must be delivered with the 100 percent certainty that only God can muster. We are brought up to believe in the ideal of the unaffected critical scientist, guided by pure reason. The scientist invades our consciousness early in life, and he becomes our alter ego, teaching us to approach life in a rational, measured manner. The goal of our educational systems is to prepare the next generation for success in an information- and technology-based society, and with that success in mind, we have been taught the fine art of handling data, facts, and figures that gain authority through their perceived exactness. The scientist has observed, scrutinized, plotted, measured, and projected every area of our lives, from our craving for chocolate to our choice of a life partner. This modern approach to the human experience leaves nothing to chance. In a culture of statistics and opinion polls, the nonlinear and murky knowledge gained through our everyday experiences has been devalued.

It's hard to argue with success. The technological edge has delivered a remarkable amount of affluence, health, and safety. Medical science has eliminated many previously deadly diseases and extended our life expectancy. Thanks to medicine in the developed world, childbirth is relatively safe for both mother and child. This is not a small thing. Technological innovations over the last one hundred years are thoroughly embedded into every second of our day; none of us is ready to live without air travel, our automobiles, or personal computers. Our stores bulge with an abundance of produce and product, thanks to agricultural and manufacturing technologies. The degree to which this has made our lives "better" is debatable; we aren't fully aware of what we may have lost. Regardless, we are highly dependent on these innovations. Because technology delivers the status symbols of society, this apparent success reinforces the belief that rational, scientific knowledge is the only knowledge that counts. The technologist—the holder of this sacred knowledge—has become our chief storyteller, prophesying a future where more technology will give us a better life.

But *will* it give us a better life? Our faith in science and technology leaves out a huge amount of the knowledge we gain every day through living, and living well requires a different kind of brain than the one our training gives us. Making sense out of all the fragmented pieces of our days requires more than clinical observation, because not everything that we experience is available to the scientist. How does one measure grief or calibrate love? Our culture's pervasive belief in the rational as the most valid form of knowledge leaves us both unprepared for the ambiguities of life and lacking the wisdom to handle the parts of our lives that are more fluid—those parts that don't respond to measurement, those requiring poetry, not data.

To grasp our complex relationship to knowledge, it is helpful to understand how we experience the knowing process. The first knowledge we acquire is deeply rooted in our bodily experiences. The forgotten knowledge we gain from being in our mother's womb and nursing at her breast becomes a permanent part of who we are. This forgotten knowledge is the sense that we are deeply interdependent beings and never truly autonomous. Our lives are dependent on others and on the earth. Our first knowing is also rooted in our experiences of pain and relief, hunger and satiation, weariness and sleep—primal experiences that can be both frightening and satisfying. This subjective experience of body-based knowledge is ambiguous and hard to define. Instead of knowledge gained by standing separate from the world, the body provides me with knowledge through union with what I am encountering, whether it is my mother, water, or my toes. It's this intuitive knowledge that has come to lack cultural authority.

A result of a narrow view of knowledge is that our ability to make sense of a large portion of our everyday experience evaporates, creating the gulf we feel between the knowledge we are trained to handle and the knowledge that emerges from our daily living. We may master the art of the deal but are unable to maintain meaningful relationships. We may understand financial statements but are unable to understand what drives us to spend. Counting calories with the precision of a chemist, we are unable to tune in to the nurturing power of a shared meal. Armed with a great deal of technical know-how, we find ourselves having difficulty managing the ebb and flow of our lives. An anxious and dissonant life is a result.

This split between rational and intuitive knowledge is also invoked in another cultural division between mind and body. The body and mind can never be fully detached from one another. Reason and intuition work in the same way. They are never truly separate. Nevertheless, because our culture values rational knowledge over intuitive knowledge, women find themselves at a disadvantage. This isn't because women aren't capable of rational thinking or are in some way more intuitive, but because women's rational knowledge has historically been questioned and is, therefore, suspect. (We will explore this cultural bias against feminine knowledge later.) In turn, women have internalized this perception of female knowledge, fostering self-doubt and affecting how a woman presents her ideas.

The divorce of intuition and rational knowledge has implications for what we come to believe about God. As we connect our embodied experience to something bigger than ourselves, we find coherence and meaning. This is largely a spiritual process. Ultimately, the split between reason and intuition that is present in our culture allows neither women nor men to be full spiritual knowers. The possibility of healing this breach promises a foundation on which to build authentic and coherent lives.

God's-Eye View

Our attempts at a holistic way of knowing are also jeopardized by our day-to-day experience in a mass communication culture. Mass media play a significant role in giving us a viewpoint we trust. In a highly mobile society we live farther from our families. We don't stay put long enough to develop the long-term trusting relationships we need. Television and the Web, however, are always present and reliable. Increasingly, the electronic village has more influence in shaping our aspirations than any actual place or community. In a mass media culture, whether it's our view of beauty, food, or the meaning of a car, our perspectives are increasingly shaped by the latest ad.

Our inundation by media creates a sharp contrast to my own memories of an early childhood in Buenos Aires, with only the occasional and faint sound of a male radio voice; television was a fantasy in store windows. Silence was often my only companion and a natural friend to childhood day-dreams. Now a color screen projects CNN in many public and private spaces, providing a continual numbing hum in the background of our lives. In any large American city there is hardly a place where you aren't forced to listen to piped-in music or talk radio. It seems that no mall, gas station, grocery store, or restaurant is immune to the intruding presence of blaring music or flickering video monitors. Grocery shopping includes constant and annoying music, interrupted only by a warm but authoritative voice exhorting us to do monthly breast self-exams. After a day of e-mail and phone input, we simply have no place to think or reflect. We literally can't hear ourselves think. The constant presence of both physical and mental *noise*—a word derived from the Latin for "nausea"—is making us spiritually, if not physically, sick.

The voice of the friendly media-based expert has become omnipresent. Entering our homes and offices, experts attempt to interpret not only the geopolitical balance but also the meaning of everything, presenting scientific-sounding information about every detail of our lives, from what we eat to how we work. Experts on morning shows explain our low energy levels and analyze our inability to get a good night's sleep. We place such a high premium on these values-clarifiers that they become celebrities. While Oprah tells us what she knows "for sure," we're left to wonder if we know anything at all. How else to explain the meteoric rise of Dr. Phil? We are desperate for somebody to cut through all the cultural noise and provide some clarity, which Dr. Phil does in that folksy way that reminds us of simpler times when advice was dispensed over backyard fences. His authoritative tone assures us. It seems that, finally, somebody knows what to do, because we often feel like we don't.

Mass communication has finally given us a Cartesian, god's-eye view—a detached and objective view of the world, cut off from the reality that we experience. We are inundated with information parading as knowledge and knowledge imitating wisdom. It's easy to become electronic voyeurs who live through the characters and advisers on the screen. Instead of agents that act and speak in the world, we find it easier to become information junkies and consumers of facts. Less and less of our thinking is a result of our own reflection and wrestling with life, which we increasingly ignore, and more of our thinking is shaped by what is offered to us electronically. The distance between our everyday reality and the world the media interprets reinforces our feeling of disconnection, shaking our confidence in what we know. It has become exceedingly hard in this cultural environment to own our thinking and to hear the rhythm of our bodies and life.

Personal Propaganda

With overwhelming cultural noise drowning out the wisdom that is emerging from our lives, we need help to hear the undercurrents. Our lives are fragmented by overused BlackBerries, competing family and career agendas, and undertended spiritual needs. No wonder Allison Pearson's novel *I Don't Know How She Does It* became a national bestseller. The idea that attempting to do it all is wreaking havoc on our lives resonates with many of us. Overcome by the sheer volume of choices regarding what or whom to believe, we are having a tougher time choosing between designer labels and spiritual paths. Instead of unplugging from the adrenalin-producing machine our lives have become, we choose to turn to a "life expert" to help us untangle these competing agendas.

The contemporary woman's ideal life not only includes the expected high-power career but also the pursuit of the perfect body and satisfying emotional life—an endeavor that requires an entire collection of experts to help her get everything she needs. Women are now big consumers of professional advice. (Witness the $150-an-hour personal coach to help you reach your life goals and the therapist who helps decipher your emotional resistance to success.) I don't want to demonize professional guides, but it's important to recognize that many more of us are *paying* therapists to help us pay attention to our lives *at the very same time* our everyday surroundings continue to sabotage their work. Suffering from twice the rates of depression as men, women are swimming in a sense of inadequacy, and professional "helpers" are there to soothe us. We hire life coaches, spiritual directors, psychotherapists, and personal trainers. Add innumerable self-help books, seminars, and the advice columns in most women's magazines. We can't get enough direction.

Our history of seeking advice from "the expert" started in the nineteenth century with America's love affair with science. Science became the path to solving our human ills. The expert, usually a male with scientific authority, provided middle- and upper-middle-class women with direction on how to mother, keep house, and fulfill their wifely duties. The authority on what was best for domestic life shifted from a wise woman in the community to the detached scientist. Women began to seek help from the expert—someone armed with scientific measurements of our condition that would solve our problems. In this way, nineteenth-century science began to unravel the old ways in which women passed on accumulated wisdom to subsequent generations of women[5]—thousands of years of human experience wiped clean by the demands of the scientific method.

Experts today operate much as priests, sages, and religious recluses did in the past: they help us do the self-reflective work we simply don't have time or room to do. Although this is necessary for many of us, the reality is that, for the most part, these experts are not present with us in the daily grind. They do not participate in the moments that fill us with anxiety. Instead, they act as mediators between our lives and ourselves. They use their special knowledge to help us negotiate the difference between our own mess and the promise of being whole. We need them more than ever.

Our reliance on experts may leave us not just with a diminished bank account but also with the inability to listen to the emotional and spiritual tremors that shake each other's lives. What was once thought of as a communal responsibility is now seen as an individual problem to be solved by individual means. Friends and family are scarce or are as confused as we are. The friend who used to hear us out for hours may now be too busy going from one appointment to another, paying for a listening ear. Wisdom that is passed from one generation to the next is giving way to clinical advice isolated from the rest of our lives. Rather than confiding in a friend or neighbor who knows us, we turn to someone armed with statistics, studies, and science. For some lonely souls, the most significant relationships are mediated by money. The truth is that for many, the offices of professional therapists are the only safe places, reflecting weaker communal ties.

Our culture's expert-mediated knowledge reminds me of the children of Israel before Mount Sinai. God was willing to speak with the people of Israel directly, but they refused the opportunity. They preferred that someone with prophetic credentials ascend the mountaintop to speak to God, then come back down and tell them what God had said. God seemed too large and too inaccessible for them. In the same way, we can find our lives too mysterious and incomprehensible, so we seek out the expert.

All this individualized guidance has to be sorted out. Do you listen to your therapist who wants you to embrace the child within or to your spiritual director who wants you to reach out to God? Does clinical advice lead to self-knowledge and true wisdom? Are we really better off emotionally and spiritually than our foremothers, who relied on each other? With ever more information, education, and experts at our beck and call, we are still experiencing a crisis of knowing and a dearth of wisdom.

Our deeply held ideas about what counts as legitimate knowledge, the noise of an intruding culture, and our dependency on experts hide a lack of self-knowledge and distract us from what we might already know. Finding a way to silence a noisy world might open us up to hearing what our own lives already tell us. In the stillness we may come face-to-face with our need. For many of us, this might be the most frightening prospect of all.

Wisdom's Call

So what is to become of the womanly wisdom known as intuition we hear so much about? That reliable standby when you don't know what else to do? Women today are using their cultural influence to reclaim intuition as a valid form of knowing. Some of us are coming to believe that the connected way of knowing that has been part of woman's culture is not only valuable, but it is essential to our survival as human beings. The dominant technological edge is being challenged by the intuitive edge, and women are leading the way in this.

Dusty from years of neglect, intuition is coming into its own as a legitimate source of knowledge among women and men. It is, however, being co-opted and adapted to the market. If there is money in it, you can believe business will find a way to capitalize on it—a prime example being Estee Lauder's men's fragrance called Intuition. Book titles such as *Practical Intuition* and *Intuition: Knowing Beyond Logic* demonstrate our interest in exploring this hidden part of ourselves. No longer just a woman's topic, intuition is changing and taking on a male face. For men who are resistant to the idea of claiming their feminine side, soft-sounding *intuition* is replaced with more masculine-defined words like *instinct, gut,* and *mastering.* In the consumer marketplace, women's wisdom is being adapted for man's instinctual advantage.

Science, not to be left behind, is looking for the biological basis for cognitive differences between the sexes. Maybe women have the needed wiring for more intuitive knowing. We hear about accessing the right side of the brain—the side that is associated with sensing, expressing emotion, and constructing meaning. There is also talk about integrative thinking in which both sides of the brain work in tandem. Science is finding that the brain's ability to do integrated thinking increases with age and has concluded that there appears to be a biological basis for the wisdom of old age.[6]

Is all this talk about intuition good for women, or is it just another diversion from what still counts as real power? Women who sought entry into formerly male arenas abandoned intuition because it was considered too "soft" to do any good where it mattered. Maybe its return only reinforces old ideas about women, hampering further gains in social authority. Cultural authority appears destined to remain in the hands of the technologist.

With all the social perils that intuition can hold for women, we are nevertheless intrigued by the value it appears to give to our experiences. We are hungry for a deep and lasting in-your-bones kind of knowing that we can share with and pass on to others. In our rediscovery of intuition, we seek not to give up rational knowing but rather to gain a holistic form of knowledge that will allow us get our spiritual bearings and make sense of our lives. What we want is a *union* of knowledge that integrates our mastery of rational knowledge and our unique experiences as women. In this way our knowing would finally be whole. We seek harmony within ourselves *and* with the world—a quality the ancient sages called *wisdom*. This is where their ancient journey toward wisdom and our contemporary journey merge.

What does the contemporary pursuit of wisdom mean for those of us who don't have the time, the money, or the inclination to devote ourselves to years of studying ancient traditions? How do we approach wisdom in a technological and information age? What does wisdom look like in lives of dual-career couples and quickly changing agendas? To find those answers, we must increase our attentiveness to the rhythms of life, enabling us to see more clearly the ebb and flow of our lives. The pursuit of wisdom is about bringing together the logic and poetry inherent in our days. Instead of consuming information like processed fast food, we would gain the soul nurturance of slow-cooked wisdom. Wisdom would give us the coherence our lives desperately need.

In *A Room of One's Own,* Virginia Woolf wrote, "It is in our idleness, in our dreams, that the submerged truth sometimes comes to the top."[7] Gaining wisdom requires that we listen to our bodies by slowing down long enough to hear our own heartbeat, feel the rush of air into our lungs, and savor the memory of our last meal. The acquisition of wisdom requires that we open ourselves to the role that communal relationships play in its search, even though it may have been our spiritual communities that caused the greatest pain. When we first open ourselves to the voice of God in the world, we become more aware of our own physical and spiritual hunger—a deep craving that points us to something other than what is offered by a magazine ad. There we will find the submerged truth in us and in the world.

As contemporary women take various paths to acquiring wisdom, we need the room to listen, to name the false stories, and to dismantle what we have come to believe about the knowing process. Many wisdom seekers are venturing away from traditional sources of authority: science, the church, and male authority figures. Many more are increasingly dissatisfied with those who possess "authoritative" knowledge and are suspicious of religious rhetoric that appears to serve the interest of maintaining things as they are. We are questioning the stories that have been given to us that don't resonate with our experience or that give no room for many stories we are still living. No longer satisfied to play along or ignore our own feelings, we are looking for alternative ways to know ourselves and to connect with God—pursuits that are intrinsically linked. Instead of dogma and a system of doctrine, many are seeking what scholar Elaine Pagels identifies as "luminous *epinoia,*" or insights and glimpses of the Divine that validate themselves in our experience.[8] Our journey has just begun.

For Wisdom is more precious than jewels, and
nothing else so worthy of desire.

PROVERBS 8:11

3

FAITH OF OUR
FATHERS

In 2005, at an academic conference on diversifying the science and engineering workforce, Harvard University president Larry Summers created a media furor over his suggestion that innate differences may explain why fewer women succeed in the fields of math and science. Many people thought that Summers, as a representative of the "best brand in higher education," was implying that women, by their nature, could not access certain kinds of knowledge. What began as an uneventful academic conference soon became a political skirmish. Women seeking acceptance into male-dominated areas became anxious over the implication of Summers's statement on their careers; from virtually every cultural corner there was an almost universal knee-jerk response, illustrating our unease over the relationship between women and knowledge.

Liberal feminists considered Summers's statement to be a Neanderthal comment revealing a bias that our entire culture has perpetuated: women think differently and, therefore, they just don't measure up. Yes, there are the Marie Curies and Jane Goodalls of the world, but they are both exceptional and rare. In the largely academic debate over whether nature or nurture is the critical factor in making us the women and men we are, those holding a radical "social construction of gender" position, in which our male and female bodies have *no* effect on who we become, completely shut down any possible hope for a resolution.

Many traditionalists nodded in agreement with Summers at what seemed to them to be an obvious characterization of women's nature:—women are better suited to taking care of their families and should leave the high-powered jobs and the more muscular thinking to men. To traditionalists, it is feminist influence, not traditional ideas, that has devalued what women freely choose to do. Of course, in this context *freely* is a highly subjective term that is shaped by economics, social expectations, and religious ideas.

For weeks, experts, pundits, and ordinary people talked through the conventional wisdom about women, men, and the brain. Many called talk shows to share the everyday gender wisdom they saw in their children. For example, they saw that boys and girls seemed to be interested in different things. When I was a child, one of my uncles made it a point to exclude me from the mostly male table discussion by telling me to go play with my dolls. I didn't actually like dolls and preferred a lively conversation about current events, even if I could only listen. *Here we go again,* I thought as the furor over Summers's comment continued. The battle over what women can and should do is not over.

Increasingly, this battle is being fought in the laboratory; science is finding genuine structural differences in the male and female brains. What we can make of these discoveries isn't clear, however. Science still doesn't have conclusive evidence about how *in utero* development and the connections between areas of the brain ultimately make us the men and women we are. What we do know is that the brain is not static. It is sensitive to factors like environment, diet, hormones, and drugs. We are never simply raw biology; biological factors interact with social conditions to make us the individuals we are.[1]

The significance of women's educational opportunities can't be underestimated; those opportunities lead to occupations that shape society. The field of technology, for example, can have a life-altering effect on all of our lives, depending on who decides what kind of technology will be developed. Will we choose to develop alternative energy sources or exploit space tourism? The presence of women could change the cultural climate in companies, institutions, and agencies where such decisions are made. Their mere presence, though, is not enough; women have to stay for the long haul. Summers's comments bring up the question of whether women will remain in the sciences long enough to make a significant impact.

By now, we know that educational achievement alone will not ensure the equal participation of women. Other barriers to entry and advancement in critical decision-making positions remain: unrealistic hours for parents with children still at home, an unbalanced view of what counts as a significant contribution, and work-cultural values that are not attractive to many women. Fewer marriages and children among high-achieving women are evidence of these barriers. The personal price that women pay under the current success model is high; we soothe ourselves by calling it a personal choice and joke about how much more we could get done if we only had a wife. These barriers are so common that people don't see them as barriers. We *expect* women to leave their work to take care of their families for "personal" reasons, without acknowledging the structural barriers that often give women no other choice. Conventional wisdom about the reasons behind women's levels of participation can seem rather benign.

What isn't innocent about conventional wisdom is that it reflects the centuries-old attitudes about women's "reduced" capacity to think, to know, and to speak. Even today, there remains an undercurrent of concern over the future of the family if too many women display an intellectual bent. In our cultural mind, "mother" and "thinker" still don't belong in the same body. A few decades of educational advancement have not erased deep-seated, historical attitudes about women.

The entrance of women en masse into various professions has generated a great deal of interest in what women bring to the decision-making process. The cultural marketplace is trying to understand how women's inclinations toward collaborative and interconnected ways of relating fit into a highly competitive world. Even so, women who achieve intellectually still live in a world that has trouble validating a woman's accomplishment. Even the women themselves experience this. One exceedingly bright and self-possessed friend of mine found herself in therapy after receiving her Ph.D. She didn't feel comfortable with herself as an authoritative knower, and that ended up sabotaging her work. We seem to be unable to escape our internalized ideas about women as less capable knowledge holders.

It seems at first unlikely that this cultural conversation about women's experience would have any bearing on women's spiritual lives. What does women's advancement in science have to do with religion or even spirituality? Assumptions about the nature of women's intellect have had a deep impact on women's spiritual history because they have shaped—and continue to shape—our spiritual experience. What seemed like a purely secular observation by Summers has spiritual implications for all women.

Woman's Glory

Our current conventional wisdom about women and men and their distinctive abilities developed over time, and it doesn't easily give way to new ways of thinking. We are still living out old patterns as we attempt to create new possibilities. Before we can continue to explore the sources of wisdom available to us, we need to take a detour through a brief survey of the knowledge women have historically been denied. It's difficult to understand who we are today and what we are experiencing if we don't understand what has come before. Digging through the dustbins of history may feel like a purely academic exercise, but doing so will help us unravel our dilemma.

In ancient Greece, the search for wisdom was a battle between the inspiration of the poets and the rationality of the philosopher. In this quarrel, Plato sought to emphasize reasoning in the path toward wisdom and minimize the lure of emotions.[2] Plato's rationality did not reflect a dispassionate and cold stance toward the world that we associate with it today. Instead, for Plato, rationality was to aid humanity in pursuit of virtue: chiefly, temperance, courage, wisdom, and justice. The attainment of virtue would lead to inner harmony and happiness.[3] In this paradigm, when women are viewed as being less rational, it's more difficult to see them as virtuous. His philosophy became the most influential strand in Western philosophy; unfortunately, the connection he developed between rationality and virtue and the split between body and soul would plague women for centuries.

Plato's philosophical viewpoint handicaps women in a subtle way. His philosophy was based on the world of thought and "Ideas"—a metaphysical sphere "above" the world we inhabit. In this way Plato devalued the material world and set the soul over the body as the true source of wisdom. Physical matter, including the body, became the source of ignorance. He created a framework wherein the soul, elevated over the body, was sexless and equal in both men and women; this sexless soul determined true individual identity.

Plato sought to escape the significance of the body in the search for wisdom, and he viewed this escape as harder for women. Women's problems arose not from their souls but rather from being trapped in bodies that were weaker; women were to be given the same education, though they would have to study longer, as they struggled to overcome their bodily handicap. In the *Republic,* women destined to become rulers in his ideal state were to be freed from the rearing of small children so they could devote themselves to study. His students, both men and women, were encouraged to move from the body-based concerns to higher levels of wisdom. Plato's sex-unity model still guides our current academic philosophy: women can have access to the same education, but both women and men are expected to forget that their bodies might have any meaningful role in their search for knowledge.

Plato's view of women's relationship to wisdom is ironic. In an almost backhanded compliment, in *Symposium* Plato offers a female personification of wisdom in Diotima—a strong model of a woman who has achieved wisdom and is able to reason and present her views. In one of Diotima's dialogues, she argues that Love has two parents, Resource and Need. She associates the cosmic mother of Love with need, poverty, and ignorance while the cosmic father of Love is associated with resource, plenty, and wisdom.[4] The association of the feminine with ignorance has been a mainstay of our ideas about women ever since.

Plato's line of thinking continued with his student Aristotle and the development of formal logic, which has guided philosophers for over two millennia. For Aristotle, male and female were hostile opposites; woman was "misbegotten," lacking something that man had. He concluded that the female was not only associated with lower matter (the body), but she was also inferior and passive. The lower reasoning capacity of women stood in the way of their attaining wisdom.

Philosopher Sister Prudence Allen notes that for Aristotle, wisdom had three aspects: theoretical, practical, and productive. Women (along with others who were to be ruled) lack the capacity to think theoretically and, therefore, could not be expected to hold knowledge—only "true opinion." But opinion did not *know* why anything was true. It was not sufficiently rooted in the "universal" but only in the immediate. It was secondhand, unstable, and prone to error. Consequently, woman's true opinion was an unreliable source of truth.[5] For Aristotle, a woman's reasoning was "without authority." Consequently, he believed woman could never truly be wise.[6] With less control over her irrational mind, she should not be involved in the public conversation at the center of Greek philosophical life.[7] A woman's best path to attaining virtue was to obey a virtuous man. This line of thinking would be used later to deny women the vote, because popular understanding dictated that a husband's vote represented his virtuous wife's acquiescence to his decision. Believing that "silence is a woman's glory," Aristotle accepted no female students. In the Greek epic, the *Odyssey*, men tried to avoid the dangerous singing Sirens; for Aristotle, men were wise to avoid the seductive voice of women.

Through the first millennium, Aristotle's philosophy and ideas about women gained influence and were joined by a parallel stream in the development of Christian theology. Greco-Roman philosophy provided the infant Christian faith an intellectual framework for expression. As early church theologians were beginning to articulate the great doctrines of the church that would influence believers for a millennium, Jerome, Tertullian of Carthage, and Ambrose, the bishop of Milan, expressed negative ideas about women. However, even in light of these views, women in the early Christian community enjoyed greater levels of freedom and higher status than their pagan counterparts, which accounts for the great number of women who flocked to the Christian church and fueled its growth.[8]

Nevertheless, Tertullian railed against women who were bold enough to teach and engage in argument. For Tertullian, giving women that kind of authority was closely linked with the real threat of heretical movements. As a result, women who wished to remain within the orthodox fold were not to teach, speak in the church, or in any way share in male authority.[9] The religious justification was scripture—the Apostle Paul's much-quoted words, "let the women be silent in the churches." A full reading of the biblical text shows that the Apostle Paul's statement, which *appears* to limit women's roles, was not a universal principle to be applied to all women in all places. In scripture, we see many instances of women as prophetic leaders, and that role required speaking out publicly; examples include Deborah, Miriam, Junia (whom the Apostle Paul himself notes as prominent among the apostles), and Phoebe, a leader in the church. Tertullian's interpretation of scripture regarding women is rife with Aristotelian influences. He, like other early church fathers, subordinated parts of scripture to the philosophy of the day. Unfortunately, their interpretations of Pauline passages are still with us.

These lingering Aristotelian influences and biased biblical interpretations create a theological foundation that is problematic for women. When Aristotle's gender views are spiritualized, the images for God in scripture become definitive statements about God's nature. God the Father—a metaphor for God's relationship to the world—is now the masculine God.[10] Once Aristotelian ideas were fully incorporated into theology, the resulting interpretation was used to support the notion that males were more adequate representatives of God, and emphasis on the masculine aspect of God continued. Women were on their way to being cut off, not only from the search for wisdom but possibly from God as well.[11]

In the pursuit of true wisdom, early Christian theologian St. Augustine incorporated faith into the equation. Reason and faith together, Augustine argued, would lead to true wisdom. Influenced by Platonic ideas, Augustine also placed women at a distinct disadvantage. In Augustine's complex gender scheme, a woman by herself was not made in the image of God; however, through the marriage bond, a woman came to participate in the *imago dei*. Woman could attain wisdom, but because she was oriented toward the body, her wisdom would have different content. Man's orientation was toward the "higher" spiritual realm. In this search for wisdom, woman would have to rise above her body and subordinate herself to higher-functioning males.[12]

This thinking continued right through to the Protestant Reformation. According to Martin Luther, at Creation woman was "a most beautiful work of God, nevertheless was not the equal of the male in glory and prestige."[13] More commonly, though, Luther would say of woman that "she is much filth and little wisdom."[14] Though Luther's radical doctrine of the "priesthood of all believers" granted women full spiritual equality before God, it was not a license for social or political equality. In marriage, woman was to be subordinated to her husband. However, in spite of his expressed misogynistic views, Luther's own relationship with his wife, Katharina von Bora, displayed the most generous aspects of his thinking and a great deal of mutuality and affection.[15] The writings of Tertullian, Ambrose, Augustine, Luther, and other early theologians leave us with the implication that the perceived vulnerability and irrationality of women prevents them from truly knowing God—even though in some instances, such as that of von Bora, women's experiences did not necessarily line up with the stated views of male church leaders.

Swimming Upstream

Given the adverse climate for women in intellectual endeavors, it is no surprise that there were few women philosophers prior to the thirteenth century and that nothing of their writing remains. Women enjoyed a better opportunity studying under Plato's sex-unity model. However, in a sense these early female philosophers had to forget that they were women. In the writing that does remain about them, some are described as being "like men" and are encouraged to disregard their female sex with all its trappings.[16] In the suppressed femininity of these pioneer philosophers, I hear echoes of the collective voice of women throughout the centuries saying, "What I know, I do not know from my experience as a woman because I have disregarded it." This centuries-old cultural doubting of women's intellectual capacity has produced a self-doubt and shame in women that continues to the present.

I have spoken with women with academic careers in philosophy and theology who wanted to make it clear to me that being a woman was not related to their academic pursuits. They wanted to avoid looking like they had a female axe to grind. Their comments all sound similar: "I am not interested in couching my words and work in a woman's perspective." I wonder, then, exactly whose perspective is being presented? Is it the perspective of a disembodied "universal man"? Women inadvertently want to distance themselves from being women in order to attain the legitimacy that male-dominated fields require. Who can blame them? Many of us have come to believe that women are silly, inconsequential beings, and we attempt to put our womanhood aside in order to be taken seriously. In the pursuit of knowledge, it's easier to try to forget that we are women than to challenge the dominant male-centered knowledge base. When we buy into this thinking, we end up not owning what we know. This is nothing new; the gulf between femaleness and knowledge has been historically so treacherous that only a few women have attempted to traverse it.

Historically, to break away from this paradigm, to assert authoritative knowledge as a woman, was to risk social isolation, or, in the worst cases, even death. Two notable women illustrate the dangers of being a female thinker. In the late fourth century, Hypatia was the first female philosopher to become a prominent public teacher of men at the Alexandria school of philosophy. She moved from merely being a disciple to becoming a Platonic philosopher, mathematician, and astronomer in her own right. None of her writings remain, and her influence made her a target. Caught in the political struggle between Christians and the ancient pagans, she was brutally and shamefully murdered by a mob faithful to the Christian Bishop Cyril.[17] A pagan woman who was both eloquent and brilliant was perhaps too much to take.

In the fourth century, sixty-three years before Hypatia, St. Catherine of Alexandria became the first Christian woman philosopher. A woman we know only through legend and church tradition, she is depicted as having a deep understanding of Greek philosophical wisdom but ultimately choosing to embrace the wisdom of faith. She is said to have challenged Emperor Maximilian on his pagan religion when she was deeply disturbed by the ritual slaughter of animals in the religious festivals. The emperor responded by throwing her in prison. There she argued with fifty of his court orators and ultimately managed to convert them to the Christian faith. As punishment for her boldness, Maximilian had her beheaded. In the medieval church, she came to represent the ideal wise woman—the patron saint of Christian philosophers and scholars. Regarded as a female personification of wisdom for over 1,600 years, St. Catherine spoke, acted, and died for her beliefs. Her greatest crime may have been teaching men about God.[18]

By the thirteenth century the first University of Paris, with its four faculties of law, theology, arts, and philosophy, was established on the foundation of Aristotelian thought. The university promoted not only a formal separation from women but also a separation among the disciplines. The Faculty of Theology focused on knowledge gained through faith. The Faculty of Arts focused on knowledge gained through reason. Clerics were denied the study of medicine, splitting the spiritual study from the study of the body. The separation of these disciplines created a path in which the search for wisdom was now fully fragmented.[19] The possibility for a holistic understanding of world and humanity was now made much more difficult.

This fragmentation of the search for wisdom included denying women full participation in its pursuit. As women were excluded from the prestigious University of Paris, the dual-gender monastery system of the previous centuries began to lose its influence. This was a double setback. Benedictine monasteries had allowed monastic men and women to study together without challenging the gender hierarchy of the institutional church. These were not idyllic places for women; nevertheless, nuns, often serving as abbesses, had access to the center of Christian philosophical activity.

The most educated women of the period in literature, medicine, and philosophy resided in monasteries that dotted the medieval landscape. In the twelfth century, Hildegard of Bingen was one of the most prolific and influential of the women theologians. She wrote major works of theology, medical guides, and numerous musical compositions, many of which are still performed today. More significant was her articulation of a philosophy of sex complementarity in which men and woman are both different and equal. In these monastic centers of learning, the influence of Aristotle was mostly felt in the study of his logical works and his method of argumentation.

The decline of the double monastery system and the establishment of the University of Paris resulted in fewer opportunities for women to access the full range of knowledge available. It also accelerated the spread of Aristotle's ideas about women. The University of Paris was not merely an academic center but also had vast popular impact throughout Europe. With the establishment of the university, Aristotle's works were more widely available, and his views on gender became popularized. Aristotle's ideas about women spread through pamphlets and "preachers" who addressed the ordinary citizen, fully entrenching the views of women that we now experience as conventional wisdom.[20] Women could still pursue intellectual careers as nuns or by being admitted to the less prestigious universities of southern Europe. However, they were barred from the most significant centers of intellectual life.[21]

The influence of the Aristotelian revolution was so strong and so universally accepted that it was almost four hundred years later, in 1641, before a woman, Marie von

Schurman, dared to write philosophy using the Aristotelian method of argument[22]—an act that certainly caused Aristotle to turn over in his grave. Until the mid-nineteenth century, virtually every major theologian and philosopher saw women as lacking in some way. In response, women adapted and found alternative paths to wisdom.

Mystical Turn

As thirteenth-century theologian Thomas Aquinas was writing his *Summa Theologica* in the Latin, women of the church were busy giving their faith an alternative expression through mystical activism. Cut off from the established knowledge sources, they simply worked with any remaining resources available to them in order to know God. With many doors of formal learning closed to them, women secluded themselves in an "inner monastery." The female stream of spirituality emphasized inwardly directed religious experience, together with social activism in the form of caring for the sick, feeding the poor, and giving to charity.[23] These two faces of women's spirituality drew on what was already believed about women.

Aquinas regarded women as helpful to man only in one way—reproduction. He opined that the role of mother or potential mother made women prone to being swayed by emotion and driven by passion. During the Middle Ages Aquinas's views were reinforced, as women, in and outside of religious orders, pursued emotionally laden mysticism. In prayer and contemplation women yielded to extreme expressions of mystical ecstasy. Through dreams, visions, and trances they sought union with God that was immediate, unaided by outside means. In this way, women attempted to free themselves from the religious limitations placed on them and the dictates of clerical control. Mysticism allowed women to circumvent the mediation of male priests.

The tradition of mysticism in Christianity offered two paths—a positive and a negative way to know God. In the early Christian mystical text, *The Cloud of Unknowing*, the key message was knowledge of God by negation, that is, a silencing of everything that is not God. In the mystical tradition, spiritual illumination is sought, not through the intellect but through a direct experience of God. For women who had no other avenue to experience with God, this provided the means to spiritual freedom. It is no wonder that women in the Middle Ages would be attracted to this form of spirituality; it promised a way to escape the confines of their sex.

Women in the Middle Ages went on to give meaning to their mystical experiences, and a few managed to write down an account of these experiences for the illumination of others. Lacking formal education, women wrote, not in the formal scholastic Latin used by Aquinas but in the common language they grew up with. Julian of Norwich, for example, wrote *The Revelation of Divine Love* in English. The vernacular language and style of the writings of these women is more open, circular, and emotional.[24] Women also displayed a higher comfort level with speaking about God as "our mother" and drawing on God's attributes of nurturance and compassion. They wrote in a more accessible and intimate way, making their writings available to a larger, nonclerical audience. The emotional tone of mystical writing tended to reinforce the notion that women were irrational, however. Women, more often than not, also felt compelled to preface their writings with declarations of their unworthiness as women to engage in the spiritual pursuit.[25] This fed a self-fulfilling cycle of women being relegated to an intuitive and emotional sphere, which was then used to show their inadequacy as rational knowers.

Another difference in the medieval mysticism practiced by men and women was the body's role in religious experiences. Being closely associated with the body, women were expected to care for the bodily needs of others. This expectation gave way to the identification of woman with the body of Christ. Women exhibited a deep devotion to the Eucharist and the crucified Christ. In their own bodies women "would provide the church with a visible demonstration of the sufferings of Christ."[26] This drive became foundational in women's spirituality and led to bodily forms of expressions almost exclusive to women. Mentioned in the writing of the period are extreme fasting, self-inflicted suffering, and bizarre bodily manifestations, which included stigmata and mystical lactation. As women were silenced in so many ways, their bodies provided the only way for them to speak. As noted by scholar Caroline Bynum, women might be said to have used the body as a form of religious expression, as they had no authority to speak otherwise.[27]

Mysticism, along with these bodily manifestations, was one of those shadow areas that afforded women some spiritual authority without directly challenging church hierarchy. According to feminist theologian Beverly Lanzetta, "What a woman was able to bear, what she embodied, loved and suffered became the text of a new book of wisdom."[28] However, a woman speaking out of this inner wisdom could be at risk of going too far. Female mysticism was always suspect, and there were many attempts to bring it under clerical control. Women who attempted to move outside the institution or to move outside their narrowly designated sphere could find themselves labeled as heretics or witches. Mysticism, however, remained a spiritual safety valve for women in a spiritually suffocating time.

Women during this period weren't simply passive observers or responders on an inward journey. This medieval female piety was passive only in one sense: it didn't directly challenge the institutional structures. Women lived out their faith through spiritual movements characterized by the lack of hierarchical leadership or rules and a general tendency to ignore institutional boundaries. Women formed loose associations that allowed them to connect with each other to fulfill their faith-inspired action.[29] The early Beguine women's movement of the thirteenth century is a notable example. These "Sisters of the Common Life" lived in or near all-female, self-governing spiritual communities. They did not seek the approval or authorization of the church hierarchy. The Beguines refused to make the choice between marriage and the cloister as a way to serve God. Single women joining the movement were allowed more freedom than in the convent, and they weren't required to have a dowry to join. By promoting the reading of the Bible in the vernacular, the Beguines provided uneducated women the opportunity for religious expression. The Church ultimately pronounced them heretical. The ambivalent relationship that developed between the Beguines and the Church continues in new forms today.[30] Though the Beguines no longer exist, other groups have emerged with the same impulse.

Medieval women mystics are the new and unlikely heroines for many contemporary women as they embark on an internal journey. There was a time when, due to their embrace of silence and self-flagellation, female mystics were considered unsuitable role models for any feminist attempting to find her voice. But some women today recognize the possibility that the internal journey into silence and acts of self-negation may contain the secret of the medieval women's spiritual survival. Whatever can be said about medieval women mystics remains rather tentative; the truth is hidden under layers of culture, theology, personal psychology, and our own bias in approaching them.

It is easier to understand why some women today are associated with mysticism. The word *mystic* is related to the Greek word *mustes,* which means "close-mouth." *Mystic* and *mute* share the same root. The mystical is unintelligible. Women continue to be identified with unspoken knowledge—the intuitive, a "lower" form of knowledge that is seen as more subjective and based on feelings. There are other similarities between medieval women and us. Today, many women are choosing to ground their spirituality outside the walls of the institutional church. I have observed that even among religiously conservative women there is a distinct female spiritual approach, even while remaining within the confines of their faith. The spirituality that women are still seeking is more collaborative, less hierarchical, and closer to our experiences as women. Women tend to be more willing to seek out alternative spaces where they can hear their own voice and claim a direct experience of God. Women are less willing to settle for a rational and disconnected understanding of God and less likely to hold that right belief is sufficient. They are more interested in holistic ways of knowing God. For some an alternative spiritual path appears to be their only choice.

Even within the churches, women have a well-carved niche. Women are still in the majority when it comes to devotion to prayer, meditation, and social work. It is still primarily the women who take care of the sick, the aged, and the young. In every church I have ever attended, there has always been a group of praying women, and when words have failed, these informal communities of praying women have provided my deepest solace. Prayer associated with passivity and contemplation has always been a socially good fit for women; nevertheless, it continues to unleash God's power in the world. In the company of praying women, I have found wisdom and courage for my life. Even as more women take the academic route and receive theological education, they are still associated with the mystical experience of God. As men continue to overwhelmingly dominate authoritative roles in speaking about God, the female stream of spirituality is still seen as lacking spiritual authority.

Centuries of women being denied the opportunity to speak and write authoritatively about God have produced an incomplete understanding of God's work in the world. When the questions women ask about God are not heard or answered, everyone's understanding of God is significantly diminished. Anything less than full inclusion of women in the theological process also reinforces the belief that women aren't equal to the task of pursuing knowledge of God. As a spiritually and intellectually curious teen looking for women who could answer my questions, I simply couldn't find them; I was referred to men for authoritative answers. The churchwomen I knew spoke about God in private, in tentative speech based on the male public proclamation.

I want to be clear here about what I mean by "speaking." In a celebrity-driven culture it is easy for us to think that the only valid form of speech is on a stage. And it *is* important for the community to see women speaking on public stages. But what has also been lost is our ability to speak with authority about God in our own lives. Even women who leave what they consider oppressive religious institutions often find themselves carrying this hesitation into new situations. When we're plagued by self-doubt, it's easy to find ourselves running around looking to a guru or teacher to validate our experience of God. These internalized, self-limiting attitudes hinder our ability to understand and articulate the movements of the Divine that run through our days. This is a vital knowledge of God that we need and that can't be left to the few women who become professional theologians. But how do we, as ordinary women, begin to make connections between our lives and God and begin to speak and act out of that reality? The ability to ask our own questions and to speak what we know is foundational to our search for wisdom.

Speaking is a highly relational, creative, and world-shaping act. The act of speaking is an act of knowing; experience alone is not knowledge. We must give those experiences meaning through words. Through speaking we participate in communal life as births and marriages are announced. Through speaking, we evoke blessings, we make promises, pronounce what we see as true, and ask for what we need. Through speaking, we cast communal visions, establish values, and retell histories. Speaking is one of the most Divine-like things we do.

In the biblical view, God creates the world *ex nihilo,* "from nothing," by calling things into being. The Divine speaking and acting continues with an understanding of human beings as *imago dei*—made in the image of God. This image of God in humanity is reflected in our creative acts. As man and woman come together, in our sexuality, work, and culture building, we gain the union of knowledge needed to have a holistic view of the world, humanity, and God. In a Christian context, it's highly problematic when women can't find their voice either personally or communally. It reinforces the idea that women somehow can't fully reflect the image of God. Women appear condemned to live out the myth of Echo, repeating what we hear and never speaking first out of our own knowing.

The suggestion that women today censor themselves may be surprising to some people; never before have women enjoyed the freedom to speak that we experience today. Yet I believe that even as we gain access to public stages, we are hitting a spiritual wall that brings up old questions, causing us to ask questions like these: Can women speak authoritatively about God out of their own experience? Can we overcome our own internalized hesitation to speak out of deep self-assurance? Is the way of Jesus still a viable and empowering path for women? Unfortunately, with the church and Western history so deeply tied to misogynistic patterns, many women feel that they can no longer hope to find the answers within the Christian tradition.

GROUND SHIFT

The ideas that have limited women's full contribution in the search for wisdom have also minimized the significant role of subjectivity in the lives of men. We can't disregard how men's own life experiences have left imprints on the ideas we live with every day. Rationality does not mean dispassionate disengagement; the language of the heart permeates much of Christian theology developed by males. In *Confessions*, Augustine wrote with the full force of emotion and out of his own experience with God. His theology was based on a personal ("I and Thou") relationship, not the abstract and dry theology that later developed. The value he placed on personal experience caused him to write, "You have made us for Yourself, Lord, and our heart is restless until it rests in You." Martin Luther's theology of grace sprang out of his own anguished, self-absorbed struggles to be at peace with God. Personal experience and their own reading of scripture motivated both men.

Human experience is messy, confounding, and difficult to decipher. In the seventeenth century, it was simply too much for René Descartes to take. As the father of modern philosophy, he solidified for Western thinkers the confidence in reason over experiential knowledge. Troubled with the need for intellectual certainty, he was unable to tolerate the mental doubts that plagued him. Descartes was passionately driven by a series of mystical dreams and a "haunting sense of personal drama" to develop his philosophy of objectivity.[31] His faith in human reasoning was summed up in his often-quoted statement, "I think; therefore, I am." Through his philosophical method, he would seek to prove the existence of God and find "objective" and absolute truth. In this way he hoped to escape human tentativeness. Descartes's objectivity became a cultural mentality, affecting ideas from journalism to theology. With its bias against embodiment and subjectivity, it fits hand in glove with other cultural ideas about women.

Most of us are not professional theologians or philosophers. We are not trying to decipher the meaning of the universe or remake the world. We just want to make sense out of our own lives. History makes us wonder if the ideas of a few men could, or should, still affect us. It's easier to say, "Never mind what all these theologians or philosophers said about women." Others of us are reluctant to face this history and its implications, frightened of how it will affect our fragile faith. However, as we seek out wisdom and a fuller understanding of God, this history casts a shadow. Everything is connected and can't be so easily dismissed as inconsequential. We can't hide our head in the sand about the history of knowledge in relation to women and its continued influence. What we believe we can know about God has been flavored by this history. What are we to do now?

Historically, some women have sought, with different amounts of success, to be included in the male-centered conversation. At a time when women's testimony was not allowed in a court of law, Mary Wollstonecraft wrote *A Vindication of the Rights of Woman*, in which she argued that women possess the same reasoning ability as men and were being kept in a state of ignorance by a lack of education. Her argument claimed that rationality was a "feminine" attribute, essential to our humanity and possessed by all women. She was one in a long line of women who sought to build a claim for equal rational participation. All of us today enjoy the fruit of this argument. But this acknowledgment of women's rationality is only half the answer. What we need is a holistic, more thorough understanding of what counts as knowledge.

Another response to the attitude toward knowledge that we have inherited is to seek out, as some have done, a distinctively "feminine" way of knowing—an authentic feminine space. Believing that women can retreat to a uniquely feminine space is a mistake, because the way we come to view and express the nature of our experiences is tied up in the language of the larger community and its history; to escape the boundaries of this communal language is all but impossible. This attempt at a feminine response ensures the continued split between reason and intuition, leaving women with no language with which to speak. We could also quickly find ourselves in the position of claiming that maleness is the problem—not a place many of us want to go. As human beings, men have a particular experience of the world that is *part* of the human experience. That's the catch. It's incomplete. In moving toward a different future, women's participation in the creation of knowledge is vital. In theology and religion, women's full participation serves to enhance everyone's understanding of God. Only as women continue to gain the authority to speak out of their own experience and ask their own questions, *and* as men recognize the subjective nature of their own knowledge, can we all move toward true wisdom.

For men and women, then, our understanding of God emerges out of individually lived experiences in the world. Ultimately, our understanding of God is judged on how it presents itself in our experience. Whether we see God primarily as the dispenser of justice or as a healer and deliverer is greatly shaped by our personal histories. Whether we choose to emphasize God's transcendence or immanence is determined by our particular place in the world. The understanding of God developed by those in power will look and sound different from the theology of outsiders. In American history, the black experience in slavery gave rise to a particular expression of Christianity. The African American experience of pain, sorrow, and separation was incorporated into the religion that they inherited from their white masters. The biblical story of

Moses and the freeing of the people of Israel from Egyptian bondage became the motif of the African American slave. This story made sense out of an otherwise senseless life. The challenge of diverse experiences in any community is to find common threads across individual stories that will result in a fuller understanding of God.

A biblical example of how our experiences shape our understanding of God is the story of Hagar. In the book of Genesis, we find her as an Egyptian slave in the household of Abram and Sarai. This was a privileged household in a special covenant with God, Yahweh. Hagar, as a slave woman, had no rights, no property, and no say, even over her own body. She was an outsider with no power to speak or to determine the course of her own life. She lived in a culture where a woman's value was tied to her fertility. In a common practice, she was given by Sarai to Abram in order to produce an heir. By birthing a child between Sarai's knees, Hagar would provide relief to Sarai's shame of childlessness. The domestic drama unfolds with a pregnant Hagar and the resultant rivalry between the women. Sarai's envy and harsh treatment finally push Hagar to run away into the wilderness.

In a physically vulnerable position and with no place to go, Hagar had a profound encounter with God. God entered her world, called her by name, and promised that her descendants would be many, but for now she must return and submit to Sarai. Hagar was as low as she could go, and this seemed to be an insensitive request. Returning to a place of invisibility and silence would seem to be more than she could bear. However, Hagar's response to God reflects her emerging theology and a resultant strength to return. The account of her story says, "Hagar gave a name to Yahweh who had spoken to her, 'You are El Roi,'" which means You-Are-the-God-Who-Sees Me.[32] In this way, Hagar goes from being invisible to being one who is seen by God. Out of her experience as a slave emerges a deep and unique knowledge of God, such that she dares to name God. Under God's eye, she gains the human dignity to return to the house of Sarai and wait for the promised future. In her practical theology, she finds in Yahweh what she needs and a change in her perspective.

Like Hagar, many women today are seeking a ground shift—a new place from which we can become spiritually whole. Like Hagar, we need to escape our own story and hear God speak our name. We can neither accept male-centered assumptions nor be trapped by "feminine" spiritual history. They are different sides to the same coin. We need the whole range of knowledge and human experience to bring us to wisdom. How can we do this in a way that does not reinforce old notions about women as emotional, body-based, and subjective while at the same time affirming that these associations with women are simply human experiences essential to our search for wisdom? With the Goddess providing problematic answers and with the troubles we have experienced in the Christian tradition, what do we have left? It is as if we have no place to stand, no room to call our own.

I believe we can look to both the past and the future for possible answers. The female personification of wisdom in global culture points to wisdom that is found in a communal effort of men and women. As women have gained acceptance as rational knowers, we are in a unique position to assert the inclusion of different kinds of knowledge. Our faith must take into account the particularity of our experiences as women, as members of a community, living in our particular time. To be full participants in the search for knowledge of God requires spiritual responsibility and a willingness to speak and act out of our own knowing. It also includes responsibility for what we have inherited and what we leave for future generations—a living tradition. We will have to give up the feminine posturing we have become accustomed to assuming and commit to what we already know. Can we do this in ways that neither indiscriminately reject the knowledge we have inherited nor gloss over how that inherited knowledge has shaped our lives?

Philosopher Lorraine Code observed that the objective knowledge our culture values promises to free us from the unruliness of nature, the body, and the fragility of human relationships.[33] I believe our experiences of nature, the body, and human relationships, with all their tentativeness, are exactly the first things that awaken our thirst for God. Only as we begin to pay attention to these can we find our way. On this path, the association of women's spirituality with the body places that spirituality theologically closer to the incarnation of God in Jesus. What has been used against us can now provide us with the answers we need. Jesus was born of a woman, and his life was sustained by women who remained with him at the cross and embraced him at his resurrection. In Jesus we have at our disposal a treasure trove of wisdom. The idea of God-made-flesh can give us the spiritual basis that will affirm our lives and provide the whole community the wisdom that we desperately crave. In the next chapters we will look at the sources of wisdom that are readily available to us.

I was beside the master craftsman, delighting him
day after day, ever at play in his presence, at play
everywhere on his earth, delighting to be with the
children of men.

PROVERBS 8:30–31

4

IT'S IN
YOUR BONES

I was eighteen years old and had just graduated from high school when I took a long-awaited trip to my native Argentina. After ten years I was returning to a country I wasn't sure I knew. To me, the land of my birth had become the dreamland of my early childhood. The trip represented my parents' hopes of returning, not to the Argentina they left but to an American dream version of it.

The preparation for the month-long trip that would take me to the homes of many uncles and aunts included all the expected angst. I purchased my ticket and packed my clothes, plus extra to give away to my cousins, and talked to my parents about what to anticipate. I was apprehensive because I didn't know whether the microcosm of Argentine culture in my parents' home had prepared me enough to navigate a whole country. I felt the pressure of my eagerly awaiting relatives. What were they expecting to see when I got off the plane? I had changed, grown up, taken on an American attitude.

To ease my anxiety, my parents reassured me that I knew everything I needed to know to enjoy my visit. "*Esta en tu sangre,*" they told me, or as we would say it, "It's in your bones." This common saying expressed the belief that bodily connections and early experiences become such a deep part of you that you can't escape them. My parents' advice was true. After an eighteen-hour trip, accompanied by an overactive case of nerves, I arrived to find that, within minutes, my body language, the tone of my Spanish, and my Argentine stride clicked. I felt like I had never left. I was greeted not only by relatives but also, unexpectedly, by the version of myself my immigrant experience had caused me to doubt. Ten years of American culture had not erased the Argentine girl in me. This original other self, who had become a shadow, emerged energetically and unself-consciously. She was, after all, in my bones.

In her book *The Creative Habit,* choreographer Twyla Tharp writes about muscle memory: as a dancer's muscles learn a dance through repetition and practice, those movements will be remembered decades after the dancer has ceased doing them. The movements become part of an internal knowing wired into every muscle. If the dancer becomes self-conscious in recapturing those movements, she will quickly lose her way and "forget" the steps.[1] Like a dancer who doubts what her body can do, when we doubt our bodies, they don't yield the wisdom they hold.

THE BODY AS REVELATORY

The body has its own particular kind of wisdom. Like my experience of returning to my homeland, our past stories are embedded in our bodies. These stories sometimes come crashing in on our present lives. The memory of an emotional trauma can release a rush of adrenalin, bringing with it a wave of nausea and tightness of breath. A smell can trigger the feeling of déjà vu. For me, the sweet aroma of wisteria brings back warm memories of my grandmother's Victorian cottage, laden with blooming vines. The memories of past experiences that the body carries can prompt us to remember what will bring us pleasure or pain. The memories the body carries can also surprise us.

Handcrafted by God to reflect the divine presence in the world, every cell—our very DNA—is infused with God's wisdom. The body has a role in revealing God's nearness to us. Full of wonder, through pain and pleasure, the body is a powerful shaper of our experiences. Our gender, race, physical limitations, and beauty create our self-perception and self-understanding. Through what we see, touch, and hear, our bodies mediate the world, shaping our point of view. In its vulnerability the body exposes us to hunger, thirst, disease, and weariness. Stress and tension show up in our bodies, alerting us to the parts of our lives that need tending.

As an able teacher, my body has provided some of life's greatest instruction. Through marriage, motherhood, and illness I have learned about the tangible love of God. A nurturing meal or an encouraging hug can point us to God. The body's greatest lesson lies in its reminders of our physical boundaries and limitations; the wisdom of the body is in the ever-present physical needs we experience. The immediacy of the body's need for nourishment, breath, and comfort is impossible to escape. Yet on a day-to-day basis, our attempts to extract wisdom out of its cues are often faltering. Most of the time, we're simply trying to keep the body and its needs from overrunning our lives.

The disconnection from the body that we experience as a culture is highlighted by our attitude toward modern medicine. We live out of touch with our natural rhythm, relying instead on scientific diagnostics. Even though we have more scientific knowledge about the body's inner workings than ever before, on a day-to-day basis, we are more estranged from it than previous generations were. We also don't have the patience to wait for the body to heal and repair itself, so we seek a quick cure for whatever ails us, whether our problem is emotional or physical. Seeing the opportunity, pharmaceutical companies bombard us with ads offering relief. By tinkering with the body through mood-altering drugs, we mask our real and often painful emotional lives. The body is expected to respond to medical intervention like a machine and our emotions like lubricants. When we have this attitude, it is more difficult for the body and our emotions, which are intertwined, to yield their wisdom.

Before the advent of modern diagnostic equipment, physicians relied on the patient's own descriptions of symptoms. For all its weaknesses, this method had two strengths: one, the patient was required to be more aware of the inner workings of her body before she saw the physician; two, the physician had to listen attentively instead of quickly rushing to apply standardized knowledge. A physician who takes time to listen is a rare find these days.

For centuries, while modern medicine was finding its way, ordinary people made use of folk medicine. When I was growing up, our economic situation and my parents' distrust of modern medicine afforded me very few trips to a doctor. This experience fostered a different attitude toward the body and illness. When we suffered an earache, upset stomach, or a rash, we had our *remedios*: homemade teas and topical ointments made from chamomile, lemon balm, eucalyptus, and other concoctions, which made some kids run the other way. For my parents, this approach to health was supported by faith, not in a *curandera,* or folk healer, but in the God who had already provided what we needed. By paying attention to the body's signals, they believed that you could discern its need; whether it was the need for rest or citrus fruit, we paid attention.

Even though folk medicine often lacked efficacy, it fostered a certain attitude toward the body and nature that overflowed into other areas of life. After a long period of hostility toward folk medicine, modern medicine is now more open to recognizing the wisdom buried in these old practices. Instead of placing scientific and centuries-old experiential knowledge in opposition, many are finding the value of bringing these two together through integrative medicine.

The care and healing of the body is only one area where we experience estrangement from our bodies. We live in a culture that is hostile toward the body in multiple ways. The body is seen to be in opposition to the inner self. Instead of taking a holistic view of a person, we see the body as merely an instrument of self-expression. Because we believe ourselves to be essentially minds attached to bodies, the body must be disciplined through rigorous diets, exercise, and cosmetic surgery to reshape it into a trophy of achievement. In an age of extreme makeovers, when even the most successful woman can feel compelled to modify her body, is it any wonder that instead of seeing our bodies as deposits of wisdom, we see them as a hindrance to our self-knowledge? In a technological world with its high value placed on order, control, and self-sufficiency, the body's vulnerability is hard for us to tolerate. Nevertheless, the evidence of undernourished and overworked lives ends up on our bodies in the form of disease and fatigue. In the face of the inevitability of death, thinking of the body as a machine and attempting to transcend it appear profoundly silly.

For women, the idea of regarding the body as a holder of wisdom proves an even greater danger than its humanity. In the historical search for wisdom, the female body has been used as a barrier against women. Starting with Plato, the questioning of women's ability to truly know and become wise has been based on views about the nature of their embodiment. The view of women as having less access to wisdom and, therefore, having less virtue is directly related to her body, its function, and its meaning. A woman's body is seen as both perennially seductive and nurturing. The significance of a woman's role in procreation renders her inescapably tied to the earth and barred from transcendence. While men devoted themselves to developing their minds, women attended to the physical needs of children and others. When the search for knowledge and wisdom is connected to overcoming the body's demands, women will find this pursuit much more treacherous.

How women's bodies are viewed continues to be a global political issue. Women's rights to basic human dignity are still not universally recognized. As women are physically violated, treated as objects for someone else's pleasure, and traded as chattel, the female body comes to lose its revelatory role. Multiple forms of violence, culturally negative attitudes toward female sexuality, and limiting views of menstruation and pregnancy cause women to experience their female bodies as hindrances to freedom. In the mass media, women's bodies are trivialized and made into passive objects, as they are used to sell everything from automobiles to steak. The message is that women's bodies are consumables and, therefore, unable to reflect the presence of God in the world. In this way, the body loses its sacramental meaning and is unable to yield its wisdom. Created as a cache of wisdom, the body instead traps us in a prison of self-doubt.

The negative meanings given to women-embodied experiences, which I have covered in my previous book, *Eve's Revenge,* have a significant impact on what women believe they can know.[2] The self-doubt that we feel begins with doubt about our bodily adequacy, which is the basis for all the other forms of doubt that we experience. The fact that our bodies are continually judged, measured, evaluated, and found wanting breeds self-doubt. For many women, their bodies have been such a source of pain that they live as ambivalent tenants in their own skin. If we can't trust our bodies—a fundamental source of knowledge—and if we feel that our bodies continually betray us, then those attitudes significantly color how we view any knowledge that we hold. When our bodies can't be trusted, all our knowledge is suspect. The body's wisdom is lost on us.

THE DIVINE TABLE

As the body displays God's wisdom, so does the earth. Even as we have more knowledge of nature and its workings, we are not able to extract from it the wisdom that can lead us to God. The more scientific knowledge we have about the natural world, the more we doubt a Creator's involvement. Natural disasters appear chaotic to us; they have a scientific explanation but no real meaning. As we seek to understand and tame nature's fury, what remains is the ability of nature to speak to us and get our attention. Many of us have felt the incredible power of the sea, or have been moved by the splendor of a mountain view, or have been frightened by a storm. Although we try to explain nature's ways through science, we still feel that the earth is somehow speaking to us, trying to tell us something vital about life. The universe moved the late astronomer and atheist Carl Sagan to poetry when he said, "Somewhere, something incredible is waiting to be known." From the most primitive to the most sophisticated people, the alluring power of this "something" is undeniable.

As a small child, I lived in a heavily urbanized area with not much grass to run in. I vividly remember a rare visit my family made to a sunflower farm. I was no taller than three feet, and I found myself surrounded by fields of gigantic flowers towering over me, their bold faces, like a Van Gogh painting, following the sun. With a child's wonderment, I was struck by their elegance, and sheer joy completely overtook me. This must be what heaven is like, I thought. The most ordinary flower can have the power to move us, draw us in, and fascinate us. We write poetry about nature's beauty and are inspired by stories of adventurers struggling against its harshness. Nature's vastness and our limitations trigger a sense of awe. It's easy to adopt religiously laden words like *mystery, majesty,* and *holy* when speaking about the earth. Reverence for the earth is a nearly universal human experience; most cultures have responded to nature with some form of adoration.

In the face of this worshipful response toward nature, Jewish monotheism made a major break. Instead of divinizing nature, the biblical writers saw nature in its radical creatureliness. In the ancient Near Eastern culture, to strip nature of its divinity and give ultimate power to something above nature was a far-reaching move. The harvest, the flock, and the womb were no longer in the hands of capricious local nature-gods but in the hands of an all-powerful Creator. God, in Jewish monotheism, was seen as intimately involved in upholding and sustaining nature. Nothing that was created escaped the revelation of the Creator's power. What had been experienced in pagan culture as the frightening mystery of nature became its creatureliness, reflecting a divine Creator.[3]

This stripping of divinity from nature didn't leave it without a spiritual role. Created by God, nature was seen as infused with the wisdom of God. The psalmist wrote, "O Lord, how manifold are Your works, in wisdom You hast made them all."[4] To the biblical writers, the glory of God was self-evident in what God had created: "The heavens declare the glory of God, and the firmament his handiwork."[5] The glory of God is the external manifestation—what is seen by the human eye of the invisible attributes of God. Through the wonderment we encounter in nature, we experience the divine, life-giving power that is present in the world. The prophets and the sages used an abundance of nature-related metaphors. God is said to cover himself with light, ride on chariots of clouds, and walk on the wings of the wind. Water becomes God's life-giving power; fire—God's justice—and wind—God's unknowable will. The Jewish sages and prophets believed that everything in the natural world was created to showcase God's power and wisdom—a continual reminder of God's nearness.

Neither did the Jewish writers see the earth as a passive, inanimate object. To them nature, which was ordered and yet open to change, was God's table of revelatory wisdom. Through it they could hear the voice of God. Western science began with this spiritual foundation, as it attempted to understand the earth as God's creation. Over time this gave way to a reductionistic view of nature—that the earth exists as the result of "natural" causes, discounting its ability to teach us anything about God. In our contemporary minds we see the earth as a closed, mechanistic system that can be explained with another scientific study. When nature's relationship to God is severed, it loses its revelatory role for us. Recovering this idea is important, not only for our own lives but for the currently ravaged earth.

The psalmist describes the earth as responsive to the Creator. Mountains, valleys, fields, and stars are said to shout for joy and sing in the presence of God. The earth is also responsive to humanity expressing a mutual recognition that the earth and humanity need each other. The earth mirrors our own rhythms and suffering. In this interdependent relationship between the earth and humanity, nature suffers or flourishes by our hand. Sharing in our brokenness, the earth is in travail, waiting for the redemption of the children of God, according to scripture. As co-creature, the earth waits with hope for wholeness and restoration.

This perspective of our commonality with the earth can help us view nature differently. When nature becomes either the end of our adoration or a machine, it can no longer fulfill its instructive role of pointing us to God. In the earth's creatureliness lies its most profound wisdom. Only as co-creature can the earth yield the wisdom we need.

The wisdom in creation provided the scripture writers with practical wisdom for living. The sages' view of time is particularly appropriate for those of us living fast-paced lives. The sages viewed the cycles of day and night and of sowing and harvest time as instructive events, able to teach us about our own seasons of life. Life has its fitting moments for laughter, tears, building, and tearing down. The sages understood that our lives ebb and flow like the tide and that wisdom is being able to recognize and understand the appropriate moments. Our contemporary understanding of time is much more standardized and utilitarian. Living in cities, estranged from the seasons of sowing and harvesting, we have lost much of our ability to discern the seasons in our own lives. As a commodity, time has lost the power to teach. A scientific or industrial view of the seasons doesn't allow us to see God's faithfulness displayed in the earth's cycles.

In his own day, Jesus warned of being able to predict the weather but unable to understand how God was moving. While Jesus performed great miracles under the noses of the religious power brokers, they were concerned with controlling him with their rules rather than recognizing God's work among them. They didn't expect God to act in their own time, so they didn't see the work of God. However, the sage writers and Jesus reflected a view that expected to see God act in time and in the world, not beyond it. When incorporated into our contemporary days, this attitude of expectancy can help us see God in our everyday world.

Living on the earth and in bodies infused with God's Wisdom, we still find that wisdom elusive. We often feel disoriented, unable to make sense of a world that is spinning out of control. In spite of being aware that both our bodies and the earth are speaking to us, why can't we decipher their meaning? How did we lose our ability to see and hear the wisdom that is in them? Our basic inability to access the wisdom around us is rooted in a deeper spiritual problem. As we seek to move toward embodied knowing, we must address this problem by revisiting the Genesis story. It's in this enduring story that we see both the beginning of wisdom and the loss of wisdom. Only by stripping it of preconceived assumptions can we see the Genesis story in light of a wisdom motif.

Eve as Wisdom Seeker

In the celebrated Sistine Chapel are two notable Michelangelo frescos that illustrate our culture's conflicting ideas about women. In the "The Creation of Man," a female figure appears to be embraced by the left arm of God, giving recognition to Wisdom's presence at Creation.[6] Until someone pointed this out to me, all I saw was God's powerful hand reaching out to Adam. A more culturally powerful depiction of the feminine is in the painting "Fall and Expulsion of Adam and Eve." I had never stopped to really consider this painting either. All I saw was the majestic beauty of the piece, often reproduced in coffee-table books. The painting's power in capturing the essence of the dialogue among Adam, Eve, and the serpent overrides the details. I was so familiar with the story I never noticed the portrayal of the serpent as a woman—a detail that now looms large. Most people don't notice this detail either. This example expresses a basic view of the close tie between women and evil. In one of the church's highest artistic expressions, Michelangelo was simply rendering a contemporary interpretation of the story. I fear this is the truth; maybe we overlook the association of women with evil because it fits our beliefs about the nature of both.

Understandably, the story of Genesis makes many women nervous. In the many false interpretations of the Genesis story, the basic conclusion is often an unspoken yet negative view of women. For centuries, people have come to this perennial story of humanity's beginnings seeking understanding about exactly what happened between Eve, Adam, and the serpent. Eve easily becomes the central figure in the story's climax. Closely identified with the serpent for giving her husband the forbidden fruit, Eve, for the most part, ends up looking bad. Adam is viewed, at best, as a victim of Eve and, at worst, as passive.

In one traditional interpretation, Eve's body becomes the means by which she seduces the man into sin. Surrounded by scantily dressed women on billboards and magazine covers, our culture still finds this one easy to believe. The conclusion is obvious: by way of women, sin enters into the world. It's women who are by nature weak-willed, easily deceived, and untrustworthy. Man's fall from perfection and the reason for the world's suffering is woman's guilt to bear. Through the pain of childbirth and man's domination of her, she pays for her guilt. Her guilt has also been used as one more underlying justification for denying women access to authoritative knowledge. She is to live banished, not only from Eden but also from the sources of God's wisdom. Woman simply can't be trusted to have the clarity, virtue, and self-control to handle truth seeking. Her gullibility in the face of evil makes her prone to error and heresy. This interpretation remains a powerful one for many people.

More recently, some have tried to rescue Eve, to look on the bright side of things by seeking other meanings originating in global mythology and outside the Genesis narrative itself. Some have gone so far as to look for a suppressed female deity among the flora or to make the serpent the misunderstood hero. No matter what you believe about the story's literal or mythical truth, it has had a powerful influence over the Western psyche, particularly in gender relationships—powerful enough to determine how some women and men view their relationships. It also provokes agenda setting and agenda justification.

Let me come at the story directly and give you my own bias. I do believe that the Genesis narrative is sacred and divinely inspired and, as such, has the power to shape our lives in redeeming ways. Because it's believed by many to be inspired, it can also be used wrongfully as a powerful weapon of control. All who try to nail down the meaning of Eden and fix its significance fail somewhere. I have looked at countless readings of this story. There is always a little piece of information that doesn't seem to fit with any particular interpretation of the rest of the story. The narrative is too brief and sketchy to quickly yield its wisdom. We want to know more than it gives, leaving us frustrated.

In my attempt to understand women's place in the world and their relationship to God, I always find myself starting in Eden. I simply can't get beyond it as a source for understanding our contemporary experience. In three brief chapters the stage is set for the rest of women's history. For our purposes, I am looking for the possible wisdom motifs in the story that could help our current situation by asking these questions: Where is wisdom? Where can it be found? What is *not* wisdom? The Genesis story is the beginning of the human search for wisdom. What we believe about this story ends up coloring what we come to believe about women and their relationship to wisdom. We can't understand the significance of Jesus as embodied Wisdom without it.

In one of my adventures into women's spirituality, I experienced one attempt to rescue Eve from centuries of misinterpretation. I found myself in the middle of a ritual to reclaim the meaning of Eve's eating of the forbidden fruit. As we sat in a circle, a basket of red apples was passed around; we were encouraged to take an apple and bite into it in defiance of the patriarchal rulers. Through this act we would declare our solidarity with Eve as a wisdom seeker, breaking away from a male Yahweh who had caged her in. I had never before encountered this particular interpretation. My Sunday school lessons about Eve came back to me; I did understand the power that this ritual of apple eating was designed to unleash. Rituals create meanings that change us; they are not empty exercises. The acts that we create and re-create with our bodies do become memories by which we live. This particular ritual had a Eucharistic flavor. As the basket of apples was coming my way, I became increasingly uncomfortable. Quietly, I stepped out of the circle, trying not to bring attention to myself, lest I be seen as a traitor to my sex. I wondered: Didn't I want to stand with other women against injustice? But I felt the ritual was manipulating me into making a false choice: either the God I knew, who was certainly no petty patriarch, or women. No matter what I did, the choice would be wholly unsatisfying.

In the apple circle, the serpent in the Genesis story became not a deceiver but the inner wisdom of women—a representation of the feminine Divine. The serpent came to represent our inner voice, guiding us toward wisdom; the tree of knowledge of good and evil became a source of freedom; the act of eating the fruit, an act of liberation claiming our wisdom and sexuality. In light of how women have been denied authoritative knowing, can we read the Genesis story in this way? Was Eve a woman seeking to assert her human dignity against a God caging her in? Was Eve a wisdom seeker, listening to her inner voice?

To see Eve as wisdom seeker we need a biblical understanding of knowledge and wisdom. Knowledge as viewed by the writers of the Bible was not primarily intellectual comprehension. To "know" was to become united with what is being known and to be known in return. To know was to experience the essence of a thing. In biblical language, sexual intercourse between men and women is spoken of as "knowing." True knowledge comes by union—an engulfing experience of being taken in by whatever we are seeking to comprehend. This parallels the contemporary idea of "getting into" something and experiencing a sense of "flow." Knowledge, as the biblical writers saw it, necessitates that we be intimately acquainted through taste, smell, and touch. This is how we are to experience the knowledge of God: "Taste and see that Yahweh is good," the Bible says.[7] Wisdom is the practical outworking of that knowledge. Wisdom is how our knowledge is lived out in everyday life.

In this story and throughout the Bible, eating is a metaphor for acquiring knowledge and, therefore, wisdom. This is a very different and fuller definition of *knowledge* than we're used to. This definition provides a holistic understanding of knowledge that is both rational and intuitive.

This knowledge yields a living and breathing wisdom lived out in our bodies. The understanding of knowledge by union saturates Eve's story.

The narrative tells us that after the earth and everything in it had been created, God declared it to be "very good." This is the earth that the Jewish sages understood to be founded by Wisdom. In this new earth, the first home of the human couple, God planted a flourishing garden in Eden. In this garden, man and woman, created in the image of God, have a freedom and responsibility that is hard to for us to imagine. They have the responsibility of authoritative care over creation and freedom to eat from the earth's abundance. They are to extend the garden beyond its first boundaries to a yet-untended earth. They have a world of possibilities open to them. In this garden of God, Adam and Eve would use all their senses to acquire knowledge and wisdom. Everything that was seen, heard, and touched would disclose the Divine. By occupying themselves with the natural world, they would feast on God's wisdom, which permeated the creation. They could become wise by becoming students of the earth, splashing through streams, digging in the dirt, and enjoying the generosity of God's hospitality. They could access the wisdom that was evident around them by reworking the earth and by eating of its bounty. This wisdom was, however, a mediated wisdom. Through experience and encounters with the rest of creation, Adam and Eve would become wise.

Among the lush foliage of Eden, the Creator placed two unique trees with special significance. How Adam and Eve responded to these two trees would determine their future. God said, "You are *free* to eat of *all* the trees in the garden. But of the tree of the knowledge of good and evil you are not to eat; for the day you eat of that, you are doomed to die."[8] One tree is forbidden. The other, the tree of life, along with all the remaining trees, was open for their enjoyment. In this "tree of life" we hear the echo of the Jewish sages who said of Wisdom, "She is a tree of life."[9] For humanity, Eden is the divine table, a sensual feast of knowledge and wisdom. The fruit of the tree of life is a continual reminder of humanity's dependency on God as the source of all wisdom. The first job the serpent undertakes is to distract Adam and Eve from the earth's abundance and the tree of life as sources of wisdom.

As we read the narrative, we need to keep certain elements in mind. In Eden, Adam and Eve are "bone of bone, flesh of flesh"—one in an intimate knowledge of each other and the world. God saw them as one, and they acted as one. To acquire wisdom, they needed each other. Another important element to notice is where Adam was while Eve was speaking to the serpent. Adam was not taking a nap or lollygagging in the lushness; he was with Eve. She had not sneaked off in order to undermine him. As Eve was socializing with the serpent, she was speaking as a representative of their union and spoke for both Adam and herself. Adam's silence is his acquiescence.

The story tells us that the serpent, who was craftier than the rest of the animals, initiated the conversation with Eve. What are we to think of this serpent? Serpents abound in culture and religion, with conflicting meaning. Serpents have been cast as a ubiquitous symbol for evil, immortality and renewal, women's wisdom, and even the crucified Christ, just to name a few.[10] The serpent has had a powerful religious meaning for many cultures. In order to avoid bringing a foreign meaning into the text, it is best to look at this *particular* serpent. This serpent is described as shrewd and, ultimately, shows itself to be a liar. The serpent understood that the means of gaining wisdom was through engagement with creation and that the man and woman were natural wisdom seekers. They were wired to look for wisdom. The serpent asked Eve, "Did God really say you were not to eat from any of the trees in the garden?"[11] The intent is to place doubt in the mind of the woman about her relationship to God.

The effect was immediate. Her response reflects her changing mind about God and her emerging doubt: "We may eat the fruit of the trees in the garden. But of the fruit of the tree in the middle of the garden God said, 'You must not eat it, nor touch it, under pain of death.'" Touching was now added to the prohibition, even though God didn't say that they couldn't touch the tree.[12] God's original offer that they may *freely* eat becomes "may eat." In Eve's mind, the freedom to eat of every tree, except for one, becomes a begrudging permission. It's as if she is thinking, "Yes, it does appear that God is holding us back. Maybe he isn't so generous." Now the door is open for the serpent to directly contradict God: "Die, you will not! On the contrary God knows that on the day that you eat from it, your eyes will be opened and you will become like God, knowing good and evil." The serpent depicts God's likeness, not in terms of immortality or omnipotence but in terms of knowing. In this way, the serpent paints for Adam and Eve a shortcut to God's wisdom.

What did this first couple lack for acquiring wisdom? One answer offered is that they were in a state of childlikeness, and, in order to grow up, they had to break away from the divine parent. Separating from the parent is an important stage in any child's life. But were Adam and Eve cosmic children, or did they have abundance of knowledge and power available to them already? They knew the difference between good and evil; God had told them that. The woman was capable of telling the serpent what God had said. They had been given the God-like responsibility to rework the earth and build human society. The freedom and wisdom available to them extended to the ends of the earth. Nevertheless, they were creatures with limitations, dependent on the mediation of the rest of creation to attain wisdom.

What was Eve looking for? Eve was not looking for either raw power or power over Adam. She wasn't even looking for immortality. What she wanted was the power that only the wisdom of God gives. What made this tree particularly desirable was the belief that its fruit had the power to make one "wise," independent of God. They were distracted by the serpent's astuteness from the multiple sources of wisdom all around them. What had been forbidden was not their access to wisdom but knowledge of evil by union—an independent wisdom. Only by taking in this forbidden fruit would they truly know what was behind God's commandment not to eat of it. For the first couple, the prohibition quickly became an arbitrary rule, and the curiosity of knowing what was behind it was too much of a temptation. "When the woman saw that the tree was good for food, and that it was a delight to the eyes, and that the tree was desirable to make one *wise,* she took from its fruit and ate; and she gave also to her husband with her, and he ate."[13] Through this singular and simple act of eating, both woman and man quickly understood what wisdom is not.

The eyes of Adam and Eve were opened, just as the serpent said, but wisdom was not what they gained. They didn't become like God. Eating of the tree of knowledge of good and evil didn't make things instantly clear; they were no surer of themselves than they had been before; rather, they were immediately filled with shame and doubt about God, doubt about themselves, and doubt about each other. Their eyes were open to evil, and now they needed to protect themselves. Instead of acquiring the wisdom of God that produces life, abundance, and harmony, they became rather foolish. They wrapped themselves with fig leaves and hid among the trees, as they tried to escape an all-seeing God. Instead of the first couple merely escaping their dependence on God, the entire human race is now in danger of being barred forever from the source of wisdom—the tree of life.

The tree of knowledge of good and evil was able to give what its name promised. It wasn't the tree of wisdom. Knowing evil by swallowing its fruit didn't produce wisdom; rather, Adam and Eve found that knowledge of evil by union destroys. As limited creatures, we can't have absolute authority to determine right and wrong. For we, unlike God, don't know what is needed for life to flourish. The consequence of this act in Eden was devastating for humanity and the entire creation. What had been sources of wisdom—the body and the earth—become sources of pain and toil. Adam and Eve's intuitive desires no longer gave them clear direction. The wisdom found in their union with each other was fractured. The God-appointed task of earth tending became a burden in a puzzling world of thorns and thistles. The body was now subject to disease and decay. Adam and Eve were expelled from the garden of God's wisdom, and, as part of the punishment for their rebellion, God "posted the great winged creatures and the fiery flashing sword, to guard the way to the tree of life,"[14] denying humanity access to Divine Wisdom. Humanity could no longer be trusted. Whatever knowledge we could unlock would now be misused.

Within a generation of Adam and Eve's exile into an uncultivated earth, their son Cain had murdered his brother Abel. Eve's sorrow in experiencing evil had gone full circle. To believe, as some attempt to do, that eating of the tree of the knowledge of good and evil was a good and necessary act of self-determination would require that we ignore the wretchedness of human history. Instead of producing wisdom, this singular act of eating produced great folly. Expelled from Eden, humanity has continued to mine the earth for knowledge, searching to extract meaning from creation. In all the millennia of accumulating human knowledge, we have not yet found how to live in harmony and abundance. Instead of leading us to wisdom, our increased knowledge often yields a sense of lack and sorrow.

The first couple's expulsion from the garden of God's wisdom was not without hope, however. There remained a promise by God that the woman would, indeed, participate in the restoration of wisdom to the world. Even after all of that, we, like Eve, remain natural-born wisdom seekers. Motivated by a desire for a deep and self-assured knowing, we want to take the world in with all its hope for wisdom. Nature and our bodies are still offering their wisdom. We find ourselves still stopping to hear the faint song of the earth. Our bodies, with their vulnerability, stir our longing for wholeness and our desire to see our physicality as a reflection of God's presence in the world. We find ourselves like the suffering sage Job, asking, "Where can wisdom be found?" Both the earth and the sea seem to say, "It is not in me."[15] As wisdom seekers, we have lost our way.

Wisdom Incognito

In Shakespeare's *The Merchant of Venice,* the wise Portia comes incognito into a courtroom to save Antonio from a harsh bargain he has made with Shylock. Only the wisdom of Portia's argument saves him from the payment of a pound of flesh. We, like Antonio and our mother, Eve, have struck a hard bargain that we are finding impossible to live with. In order to gain independence from God, we have lost the ability to access the wisdom that we seek. Still, in many stories and in life, Woman Wisdom comes incognito, calling us to herself. She is not quickly recognized, coming in unexpected places and at unexpected times. Always calling, but never remaining with us for long.

Jesus, the embodiment of God's wisdom, enters a world where only a few recognize him. The world in which Jesus lived, as much as it differs from our world, in some aspects resembles our contemporary culture. It was a world dominated by a powerful religious and political knowledge system. Conventional wisdom, both religious and political, kept women on the outside. Men were regarded as intellectually superior to women. There was strict division between clean and unclean, holy and profane persons. Knowledge of God and of the world came from the top down—a virtual propaganda machine about God. Knowledge of God was directly related to knowledge of Torah. A particular class of men were the authorities and chief interpreters of scripture. This religious class had dissected every jot and tittle of scripture. The law of God had been distorted to such a point that people were exasperated with demands for obedience based on the whims of the power brokers.

Instead of drawing people to God, this religious-knowledge class barred the way. Every religious expression was controlled, every religious position assigned. What had been given to serve humanity became a burden. What had been given as a source of wisdom—scripture—became the basis for religious folly. For most ordinary people, the door to the knowledge of God was closed and the key thrown away. In this world, women were spiritually invisible. This meant that they could not imagine ever speaking authoritatively about God. Their social position, female bodies, and lack of expertise in the Torah kept the door bolted.

Jesus, living as a free Jewish male, had many clashes with the religious insiders. Instead of exercising his male privilege, he overturned the assumptions about who can have access to God. Jesus made it a point to seek out women and to engage with them in spiritual conversations. He assumed that women already knew something. He assumed that even though they were illiterate and untaught, women were still capable, out of their own life experiences, of understanding the meaning of his teachings. As disciples, the women in Jesus' life weren't mere ornaments or domestic servants. Jesus expected women to be fully engaged in the pursuit of God's Wisdom. Jesus supported Mary of Bethany's choice to sit at his teaching table and learn from him instead of being occupied with meal preparation, while Martha, Mary's sister, was wearing herself out being the "hostess with the mostest." Mary refused to allow the social expectations placed on women to rob her of an opportunity to be Jesus' student. Later, as she experienced a deeper relationship with Jesus through the illness and death of her brother, Lazarus, this teaching would become more than intellectual knowledge.

The knowledge that Jesus gave her would become part of her inner core of wisdom, which would later serve her well.

Jesus doesn't come looking for followers who are satisfied with the answers the world offers. Like Woman Wisdom, who invites to her table anyone who lacks wisdom, Jesus doesn't seek out those who are sure. Rather, Jesus comes to those who are confused and befuddled and who don't have all the answers. Wisdom comes to those who don't have it all together, who don't know what or whom to believe. While on earth, Jesus, more often than not, shared meals with the dregs of society, the outcasts, and the religious outsiders—those who recognized their own need. Jesus continually called people to his table of Divine Wisdom. It is no surprise then that we often find Jesus teaching at meals and feasts. Jesus used mealtimes to teach us how to live and flourish. From his first miracle, when he turned water into wine at a wedding to his very last acts, meals and feasts were his natural medium for displaying his wisdom. Meals were fitting stages for imparting wisdom because Jesus was offering more than religious knowledge. He was offering a holistic way of knowing God.

By recognizing that the Wisdom among them shared their table, the foolish could become profoundly wise. Unlike the Jewish sages, Jesus didn't ask people to seek out wisdom or point to another source because he was Wisdom in the flesh. At meals he taught about the wisdom of humility, forgiveness, repentance, and the abundance of God—all things the dominant religious system had buried under its dogma. Jesus came to break the hold of false knowledge in exchange for a life of true knowing, lived out in the bodies of his followers. Instead of mere religious dogma, actions that came out of a faith in Jesus would be the true test of wise knowing. In this way, for those who hear and believe his teaching, Jesus restores the way to God's wisdom.

Sometimes Jesus, as a traveling sage full of God's wisdom, would go out of his way for a wisdom seeker. In the gospel of John, one of those wisdom seekers was a Samaritan woman.[16] She was outside the accepted knowledge system for two reasons. First, as a Samaritan she did not have the right pedigree. Racial and religious prejudice kept her out. Second, she was a woman. Because she was a Samaritan woman, a non-Jew, rabbinic law considered her continually menstruating and, therefore, unclean.[17] In her own community of Samaria she was an outcast. With a questionable reputation, she had failed the test of a good Samaritan woman. Because she was untaught, her hope of gaining a deep knowledge about God that could be lived out in her life was slim. She was looking for answers.

In the heat of the day, at a deserted water well that was off the main road, a weary Jesus stopped for a drink of water. This was no ordinary well. It was called "Jacob's well" after the Jewish patriarch. It had profound significance. It was an important source of water and a reminder of the man, Jacob, who had struggled with God. The crowds of women who daily came to draw water were long gone. Here Jesus found a lone woman struggling to draw wisdom out of the tradition she had inherited. Jesus began a conversation with her by asking for a drink of water. In this act, he broke two social taboos—one as a man speaking to a woman in public and the other as a Jew associating with the hated Samaritans. The woman, in amazement, asked how it was that he, who was obviously a Jew, would be talking to her. He responded that if she knew the gift of God and who was talking to her, the tables would be turned, and she would be asking him for water. She didn't understand his answer. He had nothing to draw water with. How could he give her water? He told her that he had living water and that when she drank it, she would never thirst again. Instead of the stagnant water of religious tradition, Jesus offered her a flowing spiritual thirst quencher. Who did he think he was? Was he greater than Jacob himself? Was he so much greater than religious tradition that he thought he could give her spiritual water? "Yes," Jesus responded, "I can give you a source of water that does not end." That sounded wonderful to her, and she asked, "Give me this water."

Not so fast. In his disarming way, Jesus said, "Go, call your husband." In this way he placed his finger at the point of her deepest pain. Jesus asked her to open up the most intimate parts of her life to wisdom. The water of wisdom he was offering would seep into every nook and cranny. She had no husband, she told him. Jesus not only knew this but also knew she had had a series of bad relationships—five to be exact, one after another. She was at a loss to explain the reason for her failed relationships. Within her community her identity was tied up with her relationships with men. She didn't understand why she had had such bad luck, why the man she lived with wouldn't or couldn't marry her. Her neighbors didn't let her forget it. She didn't understand why she had been caught up in this social and personal drama that wouldn't stop.

As Jesus, with his keen insight, focused on what was really troubling her, she quickly changed the subject. Never mind about the wreck of her life. She figured he needed to know that she had thought about religion quite a bit. She had been an astute listener to the current theological arguments about how and where to worship God. She had overheard the men argue night and day about it. Jews said this; Samaritans said that. Because he knew so much about her life, she surmised that Jesus was a prophet or at least a very intuitive man. Maybe he could offer an interesting opinion and shed some light on the religious debate.

Jesus allowed her to take this detour in the conversation. He said it wasn't enough to know the arguments, to abide by all the religious rituals, or to go to designated sacred places. God is Spirit and must be worshiped in Spirit and in truth. God can't be pinned down by religious explanations and rationalization. God is looking for those who are willing to shed their fig leaves and stand transparent before him. True worship begins with deep integrity, which is only possible when our knowledge of God is lived out in our lives. Here again, her problem reappeared—the truth about her life. This prophet was getting too close for comfort.

The Samaritan woman had a classic case of a knowledge and wisdom gap. She was not much different from us. Even though she was able to have a theological discussion, her knowledge of God at this point was based on hearsay—on what she had heard in her small village of Sychar. She could articulate the arguments and repeat the dogma of her inherited tradition, but she couldn't speak out of her own knowing. She didn't own it. Her Samaritan tradition had failed her at the point of her greatest pain.

With this religious knowledge in her head, her life remained a mess. She couldn't explain her own predicament—the chronic self-doubt and the profound loneliness of social isolation. Her life simply didn't work. Even though Jesus could provide her with religious answers, his first offer wasn't to correct her theological thinking and to set her straight. Jesus went to the heart of the need—not the need for more knowledge but for more wisdom for living. Here she was, obviously in need of wisdom, talking to Wisdom in the flesh yet unable to recognize him. She was willing to settle for the latest in religious trivia.

This prophet's talk about truth and God confused her even more, awakening a sense of longing. She responded that she and her community were waiting for the One who would bring clarity to all these religious questions. Her hope as a wisdom seeker was in the coming of the Christ, the sent One, who would reveal all things. In a rare and very private declaration, Jesus revealed himself by saying, "I that speak to you am he." Here it was, all rolled into one—her religious questions answered and her confusing life deciphered. She couldn't believe her luck! What began as an encounter with Wisdom incognito, as an ordinary Jewish man asking for water, became an extraordinary encounter with life-changing Wisdom. She quickly left her water pot and, as a wisdom bearer, ran to her village to tell her neighbors. What she told them was not how he had answered all the religious questions of the day but how he had solved the puzzle of her life. Now she understood the why of her life. Things finally made sense. She didn't have to settle for spiritual window dressing.

I think many women can identify with the Samaritan woman. Religious institutions have failed to help many find God. Instead, there is a feeling of being locked out. Others suffer from an oversaturation of religious knowledge and the weariness of too-frequent ideological battles. Some of us have heard so much about Jesus that we are not sure which version to believe. Many spiritual seekers, increasingly skeptical of Christianity and its proponents, aren't merely looking for the correct answer. We want much more as we seek wisdom for our life. We want to find a way to live out of a deep knowing. With increased spiritual awareness, the opportunity to dabble in many paths is open to us. We can often articulate a sophisticated spiritual point of view, yet our attempts at new sources of wisdom come up dry. Our lives don't work, and we know it. However, as he did for the Samaritan woman, Jesus comes to us. It is in our felt needs that the possibility of a divine encounter is truly near. It is in our craving for connectedness to our bodies, the earth, and to a community that the longing for God arises. God does not demand that we escape our bodily and social experiences. Rather, the wisdom of God comes to us in our subjectivities—our experience and understanding of the world, our needs, and desires.[18] It was at the place of her greatest tension that the Samaritan woman had the most profound encounter with God. There she not only found God but she also found herself.

Like a dancer who doesn't forget her steps because they have become a living memory, she discovered what it means to truly gain spiritual wisdom. What the Samaritan woman learned from Jesus was that true wisdom and true spirituality is a way of being and acting in the world, not transcending it. Knowledge alone will not do it. For the Samaritan woman, the memory of this day would remain with her forever. Her spirituality became rooted in a life illuminated by wisdom. She became a wise woman.

At the birth of Jesus, wise men from the East came looking for him. They had read the stars and discerned the coming of Wisdom into the world. While on earth, through his teaching and action, Jesus unlocked the way for many. Others did not hear Wisdom call in his voice. He taught a spiritual wisdom that would become part of every fiber of our being, lived out in our bodies. He had shown his authority by being fully attuned to the wisdom in nature and in the body, quieting storms and healing the sick and broken. For Jesus, flowers, rocks, and sparrows were quick sources of wisdom on how to live. Lost from this wisdom that Jesus spoke about, we are always wanderers far from Eden. However, Jesus did not leave us to wander aimlessly. He left specific signs of the path we are to take as we continue on our journey to become wise women. By following the signs left by Jesus, we can find a sure path for our search. On this path we are on our way, not only to believing but also living out the wisdom of God.

Wisdom has built herself a house, she has hewn her seven pillars, she has slaughtered her beasts, drawn her wine, she has laid her table.

PROVERBS 9:1–2

5

MEMORIAS VIVAS

We all have a certain kind of wisdom that we attempt to live by. Everyday wisdom can be as simple as remembering your mother's refrain to "do your best" or a well-thought-out list of personal commitments. Some wisdom we have inherited; some we come to through the rough-and-tumble of life. This is part of a confident knowing that allows us to get up every morning and make it out into the world.

Most of the time, by following these internalized lessons, things work out pretty well. Yet there are those times when unforeseen events bring out the gaps in our everyday wisdom, and life seems ready to swallow us. These are instances where everything seems wrong at a fundamental level. For some, it can be a derailed career, making us aware that we are fresh out of wisdom. Others are overwhelmed by the emotional tumult of relationships that threaten to consume everything else. Sometimes we are left holding the bags of unexpected losses. We all experience situations in which we have the wind knocked out of us. We may have our hopes dashed by a failed business, aborted plans, or a child we would rather not include in this year's Christmas letter. One of the greatest pains seems to be caused by the failure of what we once believed in. In this shifting sand of life, we can be as perplexed as much by what we know as by what we don't know. These are times when our intuition seems to have switched itself off, and the facts only cloud our vision. When that which once seemed certain can no longer be trusted, where are we to go for wisdom?

Life is mostly a journey to fill the potholes in the road by making sense of what doesn't. We mark our lives, not by the ordinary days but by the low and high points. When the task of deciphering the meaning of our days becomes overwhelming, we quickly seek solace. Some of us turn to our religious roots or to new forms of spirituality that promise to comfort us. On our own, we create rituals to manage the stress and distress of being human. It may be as simple as lighting a lavender candle, brewing a cup of chamomile tea, or burrowing in a warm, cozy bed. Tending a pot of geraniums seems to help. So does baking a big batch of chocolate chip cookies. It's truly amazing to me how we continue in life when so much of it is a mysterious unknown, when we have so many unanswered questions; that also provides evidence of our built-in hope and tenacity. A stable source of wisdom—one that stays with us through the valleys and mountaintops of life—is hard to come by.

Building Wisdom's House

After Jesus was crucified, the people who had come to follow him found themselves in a similarly tenuous spot. For them and for us, life is the most perplexing when wisdom vanishes before our eyes. They, like us, found themselves in a situation where what they thought they knew for sure unraveled and suddenly seemed profoundly naïve. Jesus' disciples had been looking for wisdom, and they thought they had found it in him, only to be left disappointed. To these early followers, the God of the gaps—the God who would make sense of the senseless—had come to them in Jesus. For the first time, his teaching had finally made Jewish scriptures an open book, available even to the most unenlightened. Jesus had responded powerfully to the religious knowledge brokers, jamming their propaganda machine. The disciples had seen his ability to understand nature's lessons, heal bodies, and cut through cultural expectations. Like the Samaritan woman, many had experienced the eyes that could see right through them solving the riddle of their lives. Jesus had shown them the wisdom of the rich giving up power and of the gift of a widow's pennies. In hearing his sage wisdom, the future was apparent; he would lead them to truth and liberate them from their oppressors.

After the cheering crowds welcomed Jesus into Jerusalem, his closest followers didn't anticipate what would happen next. Within a few short days, Jesus was arrested, and the religious knowledge brokers had triumphantly crucified the Wisdom of God on a cross. It didn't seem possible that one so powerful could be made so helpless. For the followers of Jesus, what had made so much sense for a time now seemed profoundly unrealistic. How could they have been duped so completely? The one they believed was the source of all wisdom had died the death of a common criminal. He had been paraded around like a village idiot, laughed at, and mocked. After experiencing such clarity in the presence of Jesus, how could his disciples live with the wrenching uncertainty? How could they believe in anything or anyone again?

Three days after the unexpected events of Jesus' crucifixion, a handful of disciples found themselves huddled in Jerusalem with their hopes dashed. As they began to hear rumors of a resurrection, they became even more confused. Mary Magdalene and other female disciples had visited the tomb and claimed to have found it empty. The women had gone to the tomb hoping to anoint the body of Jesus, but what they found instead were angels declaring that he was alive, risen from the dead. The story of a resurrection was a hard one to swallow. Women were considered unreliable witnesses in that ancient culture, and their story needed to be taken with several grains of salt. They still clung to hope; it was the female disciples who seemed to have the hardest time giving up Jesus. These women had always found themselves with Jesus at crucial moments—at the events surrounding his birth, on the cruel march to Golgotha where he was crucified, and now at an apparent resurrection. What all the disciples saw on the horizon was that lost hope and disillusionment were threatening to disperse what remained of the Jesus community.

Despondent, two disciples left Jerusalem for a village called Emmaus.[1] What they had experienced with Jesus would be hard to shake off. As these two disciples returned to their home to get on with their lives, they discussed the events of the previous few days, trying to understand what had happened. Along the way Jesus, again incognito, joined them on the road. They didn't recognize him, and he asked them what they were discussing. It is rather odd that these two, who had been with Jesus, couldn't recognize his sure voice or his piercing eyes. Instead, they were surprised that this stranger was the only one around who didn't know what had happened. It was the headline news of the day. The stranger should have known how Jesus of Nazareth, with his powerful words and miracles, had raised their hope that Israel would be freed from her political enemies. Now he had been crucified, apparently not even able to save himself. It was unbelievable that his powerful voice would remain silent before his accusers. Even more confounding was the rumor, started by some women, that he was alive.

As they walked on the dusty road, Jesus began to explain to them how their Jewish scriptures had already prophesied that this would happen. There was no need to be dismayed. He explained to them how, from the beginning, scriptures spoke of One who would be sent from God and who was to suffer and die. They were intrigued with this strange sage's interpretation of things. He seemed to be saying that Jesus' mission had not been political after all. The changes they wanted to see would have to begin in their own hearts. Riveted by his words, their hearts leaped, anticipating what he was going to say next. As the day wore down and the sun began to set, the two unaware disciples reached their home with Jesus by their side. Jesus acted as though he was going further, but they pleaded with him to stay the night. What they were hearing was too interesting, and they wanted to hear more. Jesus agreed to stay with them and share a meal. In this common act of hospitality—an invitation to a meal—these two disciples would participate in ushering in a new age. With his hosts all ears, seated at the dining table, Jesus took the bread, pronounced a blessing, broke it, and shared it with them. At that moment, the eyes of these captivated disciples were opened and they recognized him. In an instant, clarity rushed through their muddled minds. Now they understood who had traveled with them, and the significance of his words washed over them. Then, in a blink of an eye, Jesus vanished.

For these two disciples, the Jesus they had believed and then doubted had unlocked the wisdom in the scriptures. In a reversal of the Genesis story, through eating, "their eyes were open" to the Wisdom of God present in the world. Instead of being cut off from God's Wisdom, the exile from the tree of life was over. For a moment, in this Emmaus community of three, these disciples had experienced one of the first signs of the church: a community brought together by Jesus himself revealed in scripture and in the breaking of bread. This ordinary meal of hospitality was a reenactment, a *memorias vivas,* a living memory, of Jesus' last meal before his death, when he said of the bread, "this is my body broken for you"—Wisdom's sacrifice offered on the communal table. Here among a ragtag band of disciples, Wisdom intended to build her house and spread her table. Through acts of faith, symbol, and story, the new community would be the storehouse of revealed wisdom, with Jesus as its mediator. What these two disciples didn't grasp was that the Eucharistic gathering they experienced in Emmaus was to become Wisdom's house, open to all who believe.

LIVING STONES

In the heart of Peru, shrouded by clouds eight thousand feet above sea level, stand the ruins of Machu Picchu. Like Stonehenge, this archeological wonder draws those seeking to understand an ancient culture and unearth its wisdom. For the Incas who worshiped nature, Machu Picchu was particularly full of spiritual significance. I had heard about this captivating place all my life. In my imagination it was much larger than what I found: a small city whose inhabitants probably never exceeded twelve hundred. Securely nested in the lush mountains, the city's intimacy is almost claustrophobic. Compared to its centuries-old legend of sacred rituals and a priestly caste, what remains seems rather ordinary. The power of the place lies only in what our imaginations evoke. Whatever wisdom its former inhabitants might have held is now gone and forgotten, and what remains is a pile of well-placed rocks, enough to inspire many scholarly writers. The former life of the city, the whirl of activity, has now been reduced to tourists and a few determined spiritual seekers.

Church buildings can have the same feeling of dead history. One of my favorite things to do in major cities is to visit old churches. The permanence of the masonry, the otherworldly sense captured by the stained glass, the creaking of old wood, and the smell of burning candles all contribute to a sense of sacred history that new church buildings can't match. Yet for me, some of these old cathedrals have the feeling of a haunted pile of rocks. They seem so removed from our lives, so stodgily irrelevant that it is best left to church historians and a few determined souls to decipher their meaning. Even as I get a glimpse of what its former worshipers must have experienced as they marked births, marriages, and deaths, these museum pieces make me sad. As beautiful and fascinating as these religious structures are, the walls of the great cathedrals don't hold the history of the living church. Instead, the cave-like hollowness reminds me of the failure that runs through the history of the church. Can wisdom be found among this rubble?

For anyone who has ventured very far into church history, it doesn't take long to realize how troubled it has been. The power mongering alone is enough to leave anyone's faith in the church shaken. I remember how perplexed I was when I first ventured into a study of church history. The troubling history continues, as we are reminded of it virtually every day, with recent sex, money, and political scandals in the church. Between the heroics of Christians who died for their faith and the inspiration of those who engaged in tender acts of compassion lies an equal amount of treachery, deceit, and misogyny. The relationship women have had with the institutional church over the centuries is hard to sweep under the rug. For every woman who is perfectly content, it seems as if there are three who are struggling. Many women are still negotiating its boundaries, holding their breath in order to squeeze into the allotted slots. Some simply give up.

I found Amy to be struggling. She had called me and wanted to talk. Amy had the luminescent quality of the Madonna as she nursed her child in the café, where she and I shared cups of cherry tea infusion. Her tousled hair reflected her mood. Raised as the daughter of a Presbyterian minister, she was a daughter of the church—literally. Since the birth of her daughter, she was experiencing increased longing to hear the mention of God's nurturance, compassion, and lovingkindness in the sermons. These attributes of God seemed to be mentioned sporadically in the church year and mostly reserved for Mother's Day. The mention of biblical women would help. Her powerful experiences as a new mother didn't seem to have any spiritual ground in which to take root. She could be at home with God, the Father, but in all the lofty-sounding words, where did a young woman and her baby fit? The new mothers' group seemed to isolate her from the larger community, and she felt herself disappearing. Underneath all this womanly dissatisfaction, she was feeling a deep-seated disillusionment with the church itself. She had lost faith in it. As a cure, she had ventured out to a gay church and found herself in a ghetto within a ghetto—a women's spirituality group; these women affirmed God's "feminine" side. The gay men didn't join them. This wasn't what she had in mind. Now she was feeling spiritually homeless. I, on the other hand, felt that the problem was all in the definition of *church*. In our longing to be full participants, we may be casting too much of our spiritual future into the hands of an institution. In this way, we deny our personal responsibility as followers of Jesus. Maybe the church is much bigger than we ever thought. It's our definitions and expectations of the church that have to change.

My understanding of the church has protected me from a certain amount of disillusionment. Unlike Amy, I encountered the church as an institution rather late. My early experience of Christianity in Argentina offered a view of the church (*la iglesia*) as simply a gathering of those who believed in Jesus. Our church buildings were simple, plain, or even nonexistent, as we met in homes or outdoors. I did not grow up with the physical beauty of great cathedrals; the beauty was in the faces of the believing community. Our organizational structure was rather flat, for we could not afford a full-time pastor. That was actually a blessing. Everybody was needed. What kept this living church together was faith in

Jesus and a common story of our faith, as found in the Bible. Its history consisted in the lives of millions of obscure believers who left no visible trace except the faith they handed down generation after generation. I exist today as a Christian because someone passed on the faith to my parents, and they passed it on to me. From this point of view, most of the two-thousand-year history of the church is unwritten because it is unwriteable. Faith, carried in the bodies of believers, can't be reduced to church councils and hierarchies. Even though these structures have an important function, to seek the *essence* of Christianity within the institutional walls is to be deeply disappointed. Those who look to find their faith identity within the walls of the great cathedrals still puzzle me.

This suspicion of institutional structures doesn't mean that my spiritual journey has been that of a lone pilgrim. To the contrary, it's in the community of living stones that I have experienced the overwhelming and exquisite beauty of the presence of Jesus. On a rare occasion, it has been in an incense-filled cathedral, but more often than not, it has been on the winding road of life, walking with another. I have found the living Jesus and his church in dirt-floor buildings in Mexico, around campfires in the North Dakota badlands, and in the gatherings brought together by Latin American street preachers. Among the Anglicans, Presbyterians, Baptists, and charismatics that I have known resides the universal church; among these imperfect women and men of faith, I found my spiritual companions. When the institutional systems have failed us, we have kept each other from drowning.

The wisdom of this living community is its shared history in the acts and words of God. In recreating the Emmaus gathering, around word and symbol, we encounter the living Jesus.

Sometimes these sightings of Jesus are intense and deeply moving. Sometimes he still comes to us incognito, and we almost miss him. By faith, as we come together as his body on earth, we can mediate God's Wisdom to the world. When our faith in Jesus fails, so does our wisdom. As we come together in homes, on the road, or in our designated places of worship, we provide wisdom for each other's lives. As an often-dispersed community coming together, we can discern meaning we are unable to access as individuals. We have the power to speak into each other's lives words that comfort and challenge. In this living church, we grow in wisdom and hear the voice of Jesus in prayer, story, and song.

This expansive view of the church has allowed me great freedom to find the church in unexpected places and to continue to participate in the essential gathering of believers wherever it's found. It has allowed to me to see God's church in the world unhampered by walls of differences and the ruins of history. The church, in both its joy and pain, is a continual reminder that God works in history through real people. What keeps this community together across the centuries, protected even from its own hand, has been the biblical story.

SETTING THE TABLE

It was through the Jewish scriptures that Jesus explained his message and mission to the Emmaus disciples. In my early childhood, it was through flannel-board characters that I learned the same Bible stories. I learned about Noah's great challenge to build a boat that would preserve his family during a devastating flood. I learned about the mother of baby

Moses, who hid him in a basket made of bulrushes so Egyptians wouldn't kill him as a form of population control. Or how Daniel, exiled in Babylon, survived being thrown into a lions' den by King Nebuchadnezzar. When Bible heroes were in trouble, something unexpected would happen, though sometimes it would take years for help to come. I believed every one of those stories. When my family's life wasn't a bowl of cherries, these Bible stories would give us comfort. When we had more month than money, the stories of God's provision nurtured our faith enough to see possibilities in limited horizons.

When I came to the United States, every Easter season I would get Hollywood's depictions of a biblical story as I watched the movie *The Ten Commandments*. In the movie, you never see God; you only hear a booming voice. What you do see in the movie is plagues, sea partings, and lots of smoke. Most of the time, God remains an invisible and silent actor. What was not silent in the Bible stories—what spoke the loudest—were the tangible experiences people had with God in the world in which they lived. This is why the Bible has captured the minds and hearts of so many. The struggles of the biblical people and their encounters with God provide us with a way to understand our own lives today.

Since my childhood experiences with the Bible, things have changed; people have begun to openly question its trustworthiness. Some contemporary minds believe a committee of white men got together in a room and wrote the Bible. Even before Dan Brown's *The Da Vinci Code*, many people believed that the Council of Nicea made the decision to exclude texts important to women by pronouncing them as heretical. According to this conspiracy theory, women were intentionally left out of the battle for the Bible—even out of the Bible itself. This may be how congressional laws are passed, but this denies the Bible's true history. Written over 1,500 years in three languages—Hebrew, Aramaic, and Greek—by forty authors, both the Bible's message and its theme remain consistent throughout. Centuries before Emperor Constantine made his mark on Christianity by convening the Council of Nicea, the first Christians considered Jewish scriptures to be sacred text, just as Jesus did. By quoting and referring frequently to Jewish scripture, Jesus affirmed its sacred nature and its importance to us.

This preeminent place in which Jesus held Jewish scripture led the early Christians to adopt it as the basis for their faith. The motifs in Jewish scripture, including the goodness of the created world, the distinction between God and humanity, and God's work in history, were all embraced. The change was that now Christians saw it in terms of prophecy and fulfillment in Jesus. The importance that Jesus and his early followers placed on the Jewish scriptures created a community whose sense of history and identity was rooted in a canon. Their experiences of Jesus and his words were upheld and vindicated by the earlier prophets. The redeemer promised by God was now revealed in the life, death, and resurrection of Jesus of Nazareth. The Wisdom of God so evident in the wisdom books was now among them.

To the ancient Jewish text, the early Christians added the witness of those who had walked and lived with Jesus. At first, this witness was an oral history. By the end of the first century, it was written down into the four gospels we know as Matthew, Mark, Luke, and John. The view that they had the most trustworthy connection to those who had been Jesus' most intimate disciples gave the gospels the authority they have held for centuries. These early believers articulated their experience of the Word—the Wisdom of God—which they had heard, seen, and touched in Jesus.[2] During the time the church was under constant threat of persecution—and long before the church had any prospects of political power—the gospels became the basis for an orthodox tradition.[3] The gospels still call us to remember the words of a living Jesus. What we now call the Bible, meaning "book," was the foundation of the Christian faith and has been seen as a source of wisdom ever since.

To think of the Bible as a source of wisdom is far more helpful than thinking of it as a rulebook or even a set of timeless principles. It doesn't tell you what to do in every situation, contrary to what I was taught as a child; I was raised with the overly simplistic idea that all the answers to life are in the Bible. But beyond the Ten Commandments bracelet I had won at vacation Bible school, I was mostly given the stories. When I was a little down, my father always had a fitting biblical story. The implication was that wisdom was in the story. They may not have given me the practical answer to my troubles, but the stories changed my point of view.

Through narratives set in space and time, the wisdom in the biblical stories is that of an often-precarious faith lived out. The characters' wisdom falters as their faith in God wavers. They are the wisest when they are the least self-conscious about their faith. The characters in the Bible are subject to their own cultural conditioning, just as we are. God finds them where they are: in a field, a prison, a palace, or at a well. They often don't know where they are going or what they are going to do when they get there. They are not always "holy" or particularly good role models. The people in the Bible laugh, cry, lose at their own game, and are surprised by God. These are real people, not straw figures or one-dimensional archetypes. Sometimes I wish God had chosen a more peace-loving and democratic group. In a mix of foolishness and wisdom, even Solomon, who had been given access to great wisdom like no other person before or after him, ends up leaving a mess for a legacy.

The biblical understanding of God is that God acts in real history. Even though it is easy to think of history as grand events written by historians, history is also personal—the everyday embodied lives that we carry on. We make history every day. God speaks in and through the everyday moments of obscurity. The Bible has plenty of both types of history: grand-stage stories of kingdoms won and lost and personal stories of tender relationships and betrayals. Through biblical history, God reveals himself to be the wise Creator, sustainer, and redeemer of all our days. It is God's story of bringing humanity back to the living, breathing wisdom lost in Eden. More than mere literature, the Bible, as an inspired text, has the power to help us recover the wisdom in our own stories.

We live by the stories we are given and the ones created by simply living. The Bible stories fill in the inescapable gaps that emerge in our own story. In the face of disruptive events, we can find ourselves dislocated, uncertain of the end or the direction to take. At one time, the adopted daughter of a friend of mine struggled to put all the pieces of her story together. Like many people who have been adopted, she felt a break in her story. There were parts of the past she had no access to—missing relatives and the stories that go with them.

I, too, experienced a break as an immigrant. To leave the story of one nation to join another in midstream feels like switching dramas in act two. Career setbacks, relationship failures, or illnesses are breaks that have to be made sense of. These disruptions are jarring because we find ourselves caught between opposing stories: the story of what we wish and the reality that we encounter. These dissonant stories have to be negotiated and reconciled in ways that allow us to live with some sense of coherence. This is what the biblical narrative helps us do.

To do this, the Bible does not portray Elysian Fields of bliss. It doesn't even do a very good job of describing heaven. It doesn't show the way the world ought to be, in some kind of pristine state, but rather the way it is. Like life, the biblical story is full of drama, pain, and lots of wandering in the wilderness. The people in its pages suffer divine silence, wicked kings, wailing prophets, the rape of their women, and the death of their children. In some situations, when you think God will come and save the day, he seems to do nothing for Israel for years. What sometimes looks miraculous from our point of view as readers wasn't experienced that way by the characters. For every miracle mentioned, there are many ordinary days captured in all those "begets." The biblical people wait, sweat, and travail through every single day of siege, exile, barrenness, and famine. Interspersed among all the trials and tribulations are God's deliverance and provision. The biblical story is every bit as messy as our own lives. This should be a great relief to us.

In most of my life experience with the Bible, it never occurred to me that the Bible might be patriarchal. I didn't even know the meaning of the word *patriarchy*. Now I hear women object to the Bible for what they judge to be its patriarchal nature. From this perspective, it's hard to believe that women in this day and time would find anything redeeming in the Bible. It's easy to point to the male writers in a patriarchal culture depicting violence against women, women who are married off and valued as chattel, or worst of all, women who are simply ignored and made invisible. There are some real victims, both male and female, in the Bible. Isn't the Bible's portrayal of women and their social position an honest and realistic depiction? Elizabeth Cady Stanton, a leader of the nineteenth-century suffrage movement, was so convinced the Bible was to blame for women's plight that in 1895, she and a revising committee took it upon themselves to publish their own Bible, along with commentary. These early spiritual feminists challenged those passages that they perceived as misogynistic. Following in the tradition of Stanton, some contemporary women have taken a stance of suspicion toward the text. They want to fill in the story that appears to be missing by giving a voice to the slighted biblical women. I think this is a natural response to the undeniable fact that the Bible has been *used* throughout history as a tool to subordinate women, racial minorities, and generally anybody in the lower classes. Saying that the Bible has been used against women is different from saying that the text itself is the problem. With its cultural and spiritual authority, the Bible has been used to tell women to be quiet, submit to abuse, and, yes, even "put out." In some fundamentalist circles, the Bible, when used in this way, is still quite effective.

How can this puzzling and often exasperating book possibly provide any shred of wisdom for contemporary women? Fewer of us have read it, and more of us think it is wholly inadequate for our needs. While the biblical women remain veiled and often silent, we enjoy unprecedented freedom. While they protect their prized virginity and focus on childbearing and baking bread, we have careers. What can they possibly teach us?

The biblical story, as seen from a woman's point of view, does have a different flavor, though the essence of the story remains God's redemption of humanity. Through marriages, births, and widowhood, these women experience all the joy and pain of being female. Like the men in the Bible, biblical women often focus on escaping their enemies and anticipating the birth of children. They occasionally speak for God and take bold action. As in real life, women are raped, abused, and show up as the unexpected hero or villain. The men are realistic, too. The Bible doesn't idolize them, either. These stories illustrate the good and the bad that women have historically experienced—and still experience in most of the world. As contemporary Western women who can find ourselves frozen in our Western freedoms, we need the biblical stories to heal our internalized shame of being female. We need the biblical stories to help us move out of the chains of self-doubt that politics has failed to unlock. When we look at the whole story and not just at what is convenient, the lives of biblical women and men help us see how God moves in our own lives.

The biblical stories I heard as a child, and often still hear, are selective. Growing up, I heard about seductive Delilah, who actually nagged Samson into giving up the secret of his strength, but never the warrior Jael, who drove a stake through the temple of an enemy general and delivered her people. I heard about the murderous Jezebel, but courageous and prophetic Mary was slighted unless it was Christmas Eve. I guess this is because it was expected that girls would be better trained by the negative examples than by the positive ones. When adults did offer a positive example of a biblical woman, they emphasized only certain aspects of the woman's character. I heard about Esther's beauty more than I did about her courage. The women I heard about were colored with the particular interpretive lens of my community.

Other stories remain the dirty little secrets of the Bible, those unmentionable in pious company. These I never heard. The narratives of the rape of Dinah, Tamar's boldness in the face of disgrace, Zelophehad's daughters demanding rights of inheritance, and the brutal rape, murder, and dismemberment of a concubine in Judges 19 are not ignored by God, but by us. God stopped to record the injustices. I have rarely heard these passages read out loud. They're too bold and raw in their demand for justice. They are too messy and don't strike a pleasant chord in our contemporary religious sensibilities. In some parts of the world, a woman's life is still considered to be worth less than a dog's; these are the stories that today's women desperately need to hear.

The work of interpreting these stories, of understanding their significance, still needs to be done. More and more women and men are engaging these texts. Emerging out of an oral culture, the biblical stories were to be read out loud in the community. In this way, they are healing; as we read them in community, we are able to emerge out of the self-absorption of our individual stories. I believe it's not until we face these difficult stories that we will be able to fill in our own. Only when the whole community faces the recorded experience of the biblical women from God's point of view will women be fully included as authoritative knowers.

By participating in the communal practice of reading and interpreting, we can find the Wisdom of God in the scriptures. In the retelling of the biblical stories, we are invited to come to a different point of view.[4] We are not left alone to figure out what is "true" for us, but we are surrounded by witnesses to God's work in our lives. As women participate in retelling the story of God's redemption, the whole community gains a fuller understanding of its meaning. The collaborative nature of this process is why reading the Bible out loud was, and is, an important practice in Christianity—a practice that is barely kept alive in most Christian circles. As we hear our sacred history, the possibility emerges that our lives can be healed and our faith ignited—a faith that places us on wisdom's path.

Wisdom's Way

As we have seen, wisdom does come to us in multiple ways. The wisdom resident in nature, the body, God's community, and sacred text can help us make sense of our lives. Jesus, through his words and acts, pointed to all these sources. Yet finding wisdom remains difficult. None of these things, alone or together, is sufficient. Nature and the body are often indecipherable. Our contemporary sense of a viable faith community is diminished, and the Bible has become suspect for many of us. In the midst of a culture claiming certainty of knowledge through media and technology, we must find a way to interpret the often-cryptic messages coming from within our own lives. The early followers of Jesus believed that the Wisdom of God was ultimately found through faith, not through poetry, philosophy, or religious observance. Neither rational nor inner knowledge could unlock true wisdom. Only the freely given revelation of God could disclose what was absolutely hidden from humanity. By trusting in Jesus, the Wisdom of God would come and dwell in their hearts.

To the contemporary mind, infected with scientism and postmodern suspicion of any truth claim, faith can be a tricky endeavor. Many people think of faith as blind, an irrational clinging to something whether it is a tradition or a talisman. We either want proof, or we make faith impotent by privatizing it. That is how we are trained. In everyday conversation, confessions of faith can color everything else. If I claim faith, the conversation is stopped in its tracks. To claim faith has come to mean that my reasons are so personal, so disassociated from reality, that they are incommunicable. To call someone a person of faith is to say that she is possibly either dangerous or out of touch with reality.

The early followers of Jesus had a completely different attitude toward faith. Theirs was not a free-floating faith, landing on whatever was personally appealing; their faith was attached to a specific object of faith—Jesus. To them, faith was based on the historical acts of God in and through Jesus. It sprang from the stories passed on by trustworthy eyewitnesses of Jesus' life and the Jewish scriptures. The essence of this faith was *a way of knowing*, of revealed knowledge and wisdom. They saw faith in Jesus as unlocking the revelation of God stored in Wisdom's house. Faith allowed them to respond to God and to come and remain at Wisdom's table.

Faith is not intuition or insight. It is a wholly other type of knowing. Faith is not agreeing with a set of doctrines or dogma. Faith is not being convinced of the truth, even though it makes a truth claim. These first disciples had already experienced this form of religion. They came to an understanding of God that was neither gained by objective knowledge nor by going within, but by reaching out, walking into a terrifying divine presence. For those who followed Jesus, faith became a personal, engulfing experience—a form of being taken in. It was knowledge of God by union. The initial human response to the experience of faith is to feel as though we are losing ourselves and are free-falling into the unknown. As we surrender to the call of divine love, we come out of our individual isolation and find ourselves in relationship with God. In this radically communal act, we can participate in the intimacy of God and of his people. It is both complete freedom and complete dependency.[5] Through faith our sense of self, our sense of community, is invested in God.

The revelation of God that faith makes possible is made tangible in the demonstration of love. Faith is most of all communal. Love, not knowledge, becomes the principle sign of our participation in the life of the Divine. The wisdom of embodied love overshadows all other knowledge. Faith is knowledge that acts in the world. This true wisdom is never passive but is made visible through the acts of the believer. Every kind of work, every relationship, every bodily act is a fruit of this faith. The wisdom of embodied love can't be gained through a do-it-yourself spirituality but is rooted and nurtured by God's community and scripture. It's the tangible love demonstrated toward a neighbor that ultimately makes the difference in the world. Through this wisdom, women and men in the early church, who previously had been shut out of the knowledge of God, became profoundly wise agents of transformation.

The early Christians proclaimed a message of faith by which knowledge of God was available to all. It's a fundamentally egalitarian message. There is neither gentile nor Jew, slave nor freeman, male nor female in the household of God. Faith makes the knowledge of God available to all, even the least educated, the poorest, and those of the lowest class.

It doesn't require a teacher with secret knowledge, tedious course work into mysteries, or expensive rituals. There is no human sacrifice or achievement that can attain this wisdom. In any society in which social class and achievement are considered indicative of someone's worth, faith as the way to know God is a great equalizer. It explains the great attraction that the way of Jesus has historically held for women and slaves. In our contemporary world, even as the powerful West with its technological knowledge is estranged from this faith, it spreads rapidly among the poor and the untouchables of the developing world. Their wisdom may overtake us.

It was by the establishment of Wisdom's house, the gathering of believers, and affirming the role of a sacred story that Jesus left for us the path by which we can become wise. It is a path made available to us by the revelation that Jesus himself provides. Through the transformative revelation of God, a band of disappointed and doubting disciples turned the world upside down. From a moment when God's wisdom seemed lost forever, the power of faith in a living Jesus has reverberated through the centuries. It is a faith that has survived state-sponsored persecution, the seduction of politics, and attempts to tame it through institutionalization and reinterpretation. In millions of obscure corners of the earth, faith has managed to survive in the lives of Jesus' followers.

Faith, for us, still opens the way to a wisdom that challenges the world. Faith is not passive. Faith always takes a suspicious stance toward systems that continue to offer power through knowledge, as the serpent did. It would cause the Apostle Paul to ask, "Where are the philosophers? Where are the experts? Where are the debaters of this age?"[6] For the Apostle Paul, God had overthrown human knowledge as folly. By placing human knowledge at the service of faith, wisdom emerges. Faith provides us with a way to challenge not only the world's knowledge machine but also the community of believers when it departs from wisdom's way, and to finally see ourselves in the pages of the Bible. As we listen to the words of Jesus, we draw closer to a wisdom that can help us to act and speak out of a deep knowing. More radical than intuition or rational knowledge, faith opens the door to a living wisdom.

Wisdom is brilliant, she never fades. By those who love her, she is readily seen, by those that seek her, she is readily found.

THE BOOK OF WISDOM, 6:12

6

YOUR OWN PERSONAL JESUS

Over *mojitos* at one of my favorite Latin cafés, Claire and I sat sharing our individual survival strategies. Claire told me how in the previous six months she had swallowed her pride and returned to the church of her childhood. In pursuit of wisdom, she had gone through a time of spiritual avoidance and dabbled unconvincingly in Buddhism, but now she was back. She still had to do mental gymnastics in order to get through the creeds and the Eucharist; she found the liturgical reference to "sacrifice for sins" to be especially disconcerting. But she pressed on.

I sensed that the finer details of the faith violated her deepest sensibilities. Hearing the feminine voices of women clergy certainly helped, but she wasn't completely comfortable in the services yet. This led to my questions: Why recite a confession you don't believe? Why participate in rituals that distress you? Wouldn't it be more honest to simply leave and start over somewhere else? "No, it's the tradition I've come from," she said. Besides, she loved the music. During her hiatus from the church, it was the music that she had missed. A Christmas sing-along of Handel's *Messiah* had brought her back. The familiarity of the smells and sounds in the old chapel and the sense of connectedness to history had restored her sense of calling. Though she had never abandoned her belief in Jesus, her relationship to Christianity remained shaky.

Many women have a complex relationship with the Christian tradition. On the one hand, they may crave its solidity, its sense of permanence in a constantly changing world. On the other hand, its apparent lack of fluidity, its unwillingness to change its fundamental doctrines, can get under the skin of many would-be Jesus followers. To resolve this conflict, Claire was doing her own exploration every Tuesday night with other women in an informal group they called the Magdalene circle. She asked me if I had read the gospel of Thomas, which I had, and told me how it had added something to her understanding of Jesus. She was convinced that somehow orthodox Christianity had misunderstood him. She was searching beyond the dogma of the church and exploring inner wisdom—searching for the kingdom of God within. Where inner exploration would lead her, she didn't know. The process was centered on understanding her experience as a woman and learning to trust her inner voice. She hoped to find a long-term, satisfying resolution to her ambivalent relationship to the church.

In the previous chapters, we have looked at several sources of wisdom: the natural world, our bodies, scripture, and the community of faith. Now it's time to consider one of the most popularly understood sources of wisdom: the inward journey. This is the attempt to find, under layers of conditioning, an authentic true self—a more confident, more powerful version of self. It's a search for an inner, divine self that transcends the dictates of the community. This raises the question: Is the self the final wise one? Are we our own best spiritual guide? Can self-doubt be replaced with an inward-dwelling wisdom?

A LOST JESUS

Now in charge of their own spiritual lives, women have returned to the inbound journey of the centuries as a means of connecting to the Divine. In this new millennium, the spiritual activist has replaced the social and political activist of the twentieth century as the new female hero. To "doctor," "lawyer," or "CEO," we can now include the title "wise woman." Women who had given up their mother's religion for the rewards of secular rationality are now returning to the quintessential female spiritual journey—the journey to find the Divine within us. Because many women feel they are made invisible by the Bible and its interpretations, excluded from speaking authoritatively about God, and placed at odds with their bodies, the inward path to wisdom may be the only route left to God. This inner path is what is expected from women. Many see this path as an opportunity to define God for themselves and gain an inner authority by which to live. In a spiritually deafening world where there hardly remains any space in which to hear the voice of God, some believe we might just find it inside ourselves.

For many feeling distrustful of traditional religion, relying on their own spiritual wits to help them find their way appears to be a viable option. In a culture that values only certain types of knowledge and questions women's ability to truly know, articles and books attempt to assure us there is wisdom dwelling deep within. The inward path promises healing for the crisis of knowing and deep-seated self-doubt. In the mystical search, many have come to believe that wisdom can be drawn like water from the dark well of the soul. Becoming aware of the wisdom within us and overcoming the ignorance of our divinity provides ultimate healing. But is it really this easy?

Only women of relative affluence can set off on this inner path, as it requires considerable time, energy, and disposable income. We expend all three on spiritual self-help books, seminars, and guides of all stripes. There are millions of Web sites alone that cater to every variety of woman, from passionate singles to stressed-out moms—all trying to find themselves under all of life's complexities. Women are attempting to journal, meditate, and drum themselves from under the piles of expectations. From dream work to breathing work, every technique and method possible is available for this journey. More than one of my friends could easily pass for a professional spiritual seeker on her way to becoming enlightened. Such seekers are open to any new technique or experience that promises to open the door to another room in their souls. A friend in a reflective mood may spend thousands of dollars going to eco-retreats, soul spas, and seminars featuring the latest in traveling gurus. There she embraces personal transformation while eating gourmet vegetarian meals against the backdrop of a mystical mountain view. She returns, elated with new-convert fever, having found the key to unlock her life's secrets. The next week, she moves on to something new. The underpinnings and themes of her life remain unchanged.

For many women in the rest of the world—never mind those throughout history—the spiritual pursuit is deeply connected to putting food on the table, ushering a child through an illness, and securing their basic human dignity. To a large percentage of the world's women, excavation of the self is meaningless when everyday survival and dignity are at stake. On one occasion I was asked to speak to a group of women diplomats from around the world. They came in everything from colorful African dress to the drab apparel of Eastern Europe's emerging nations. Asian and South American women joined us, too. They were among the world's brightest and best-educated women, and their soulful interest in spirituality, regardless of their religious heritage, seemed to hang on the concrete needs of their communities.

Among this most privileged group, the spiritual questions reflected women's global search for human dignity and freedom from oppression. In comparison to our Western sophisticated souls, their approach to spirituality was robust with real purpose. Instead of the self-absorption we often see in much of the West, they were concerned with the larger questions of their communities. The difference was remarkable. When many of the world's women pray, they aren't seeking the Divine within; rather, they are longing for concrete manifestations of God in their communities and lives. This attitude gives way to the possibility of a vibrant, active faith as they come to know God through tangible demonstrations of love. It makes me wonder what the point of my own spiritual journey actually is.

Women in our society are not on an inner journey all by themselves. Women's search for wisdom within dovetails with Western culture's increased suspicion of traditional religious institutions and troublesome dogma. For many, part of this troubling dogma is the definition of Jesus. Some grew up with a Jesus Christ who was so highly exalted at the right hand of God that he completely lost his humanity. That Jesus wouldn't get down here with us in our mess. It's hard to imagine this "Lord of lords," who lives in a cathedral, sitting down and sharing a meal with us. For women who have been systematically excluded from full participation in church life, this experience of Jesus can be much more pronounced. Others have had a cursory introduction to Jesus, and while his aura was attractive, they found the overall Christian package seriously lacking an affinity to women's needs; they see a large gap between Jesus and the religion that claims him. Many are trying to find a lost Jesus who fits feminist-enhanced sensibilities and makes a suitable traveling companion for the inbound journey.

The Jesus of Nazareth written about in the gospel narratives is harder to find among the proliferation of Jesuses in pop culture. When anyone mentions Jesus, I wonder what Jesus the person is talking about. I remember in the early seventies the uproar over the movie *Jesus Christ Superstar.* In some fundamentalist circles this movie was nothing short of blasphemy. It would surely bring the end of America as we knew it. Not only did the world not end, few people think anything about a movie like this now, because we have come to accept that we all have our own versions of Jesus, whether he's the pop version or not. We now have Martin Scorsese's "I am just like you" Jesus in *The Last Temptation of Christ,* Mel Gibson's suffering Jesus in *The Passion of the Christ,* Anne Rice's imaginative-child Jesus, and Pat Robertson's Rambo Jesus, with the companion action-figure Jesus. For those more practically inclined, there is Jesus as an expert. In a world where knowledge is seen as the way to salvation and profit, Jesus as a management guru or life coach is appealing. Even John Shelby Spong, the now-retired and infamous Episcopal bishop who advocates a complete redefinition of Christianity to better fit our new knowledge base, is not willing to dispense with Jesus.

The deconstruction of the Jesus whose life is as recorded in the gospels ensures that at some point his own words will become a problem, and we are quickly on our way to new Christianities. A Jesus Christ who minced no words, saw through people's self-deception, and claimed to be the unique Son of God is a rare find. Contemporary and popular renderings of Jesus too often strip him of his divinity. Jesus becomes merely a spiritual prodigy. In this way he goes from being the redeemer of the world to being a fully self-actualized master. The proliferation of Jesus clones in popular culture has virtually ensured that everyone can find a Jesus who best suits them. Any politician, celebrity, or cultural provocateur can claim him. The implication for wisdom seekers is that if the Jesus of the gospels is the embodiment of Divine Wisdom, identifying him in the crowd becomes much more difficult.

The truth is, we cannot avoid having our own personal version of Jesus. Because we bring our own histories to our encounter with him, we each come to hear and experience him differently. This was true of the earliest disciples, and so it is with us. The life and teachings of Jesus will affect each one of us in a different way. We may experience him as healer, Savior, or Prince of Peace. Yet it's in the fullness of the Jesus written about in the gospels—the knowledge of a historically experienced Jesus—that our hearts and minds will be enlarged. We can't remain with a safe Jesus. Otherwise, he serves only to validate and affirm our experience but never to change or challenge our lives.

Much of our contemporary notions of Jesus, his message, and our attitude toward the inner search for wisdom have their roots in the ancient Gnostic tradition. The Gnostic movement arose in juxtaposition to what became known as Orthodox Christianity; it is often identified as Christian in origin. Today, one of the greatest popular influences on how we think about Jesus has been Elaine Pagels's widely read *The Gnostic Gospels*. Attaching the word *gospel* to anything gives it considerable weight. We expect something to be reliable when it is declared to be the "gospel truth." In her book, Pagels manages to bring popular attention to something that had remained enclosed in the lofty towers of scholarly battles. The 1945 Nag Hammadi discovery of thirteen papyrus books in Egypt contained a treasure trove of Gnostic writings. The resulting events make for a captivating "Indiana Jones" adventure. Here we have the makings of a real mystery: ancient books lost for centuries discovered by accident, the intrigue of black-market dealers, and finally, biblical scholars eager for some new evidence for the historical Jesus. In the popular imagination, Jesus would never be the same.

It doesn't take much reading to figure out how perfectly suited the ancient Gnostic belief system is to our own notions of spirituality. There are very few people running around today calling themselves Gnostics. However, Gnostic ideas are very much part of today's spiritual climate. Instead of the mediated wisdom that relies on faith in Jesus, the Gnostics sought an independent wisdom resident in the spiritual seeker. The Gnostics believed that they were heirs of a secret tradition passed on by Jesus to a select few. Their second-century writings claimed to be authentic records of the deeds and words of Jesus.[1] Whether the writings that survived were spiritual musings of imaginative leaders or purely works of fiction, they continue to fuel speculation about the true nature of Jesus and his teaching.

Like contemporary gurus and spiritual experts, Gnostics leaders were the holders of secret *gnosis,* or insight. This teaching held that one could attain a direct and absolute knowledge of the Divine through an internal experience. This knowledge of God extended beyond that attained through the natural world, scripture, or the community of believers. It transcended the creeds and symbols of the then-emerging Orthodox community. For the Gnostics, salvation came through secret knowledge available to the initiated. Ignorance (defined as lacking knowledge of our own divinity), not sin, was the real problem. This knowing self was said to be the God within. The self was not flawed but was the essence of God. By knowing one's true and pure self, one could come to know God—the self and God being interchangeable. According to Pagels, "To know oneself, at the deepest level, is simultaneously to know God; this is the secret of gnosis."[2] This knowledge of the self was not rooted in our bodily experiences in a material world. It was a detached self, free of social and bodily limitations, through which we would come to truly experience ourselves as divine. Today, we still view spirituality largely as an ethereal experience.

Having rejected the Jewish scriptures with its wise Creator, the Gnostics believed the world of matter and body was a product of evil forces. In one myth, Sophia, a divine feminine power, initially brought forth a defective world. In order to correct her error, she then created the balancing male demiurge—the creator-God of Israel. As one with derived power, Yahweh was delusional and thought of himself as all-powerful.[3] As a result of this primordial mistake, the material world was full of ignorance and error. Wisdom could not be found here. Spiritual progress was measured by one's ability to escape to the higher spiritual realms of light and truth. This was done through attaining stages of spiritual advancements, as Jesus had done. In this worldview, the coming of Jesus as the Christ, his death, and his resurrection were not unique historical events but were symbolic of inward experiences[4]—experiences that could be relived by each of us, allowing all to become a "Christ."

The suspicion and often-outright rejection of the body and the material world in Gnostic ideas make those notions strange candidates for revival among contemporary women. The second century, permeated as it was with Gnostic thought, was not exactly a golden age for women. Even though women were prominent in Gnostic circles and texts, as a whole, Gnosticism took the negative view of women to a whole new level. Because Gnostics had a low view of the body, women's role in reproduction made them agents of a conspiracy to keep humanity enslaved.[5] In Gnostic texts, we see repeated references to women and womanhood as problems. In the *Gospel of Thomas* we find this: "Simon Peter said to them, 'Make Mary leave us, for females don't deserve to live.' Jesus said, 'Look, I will guide her to make her male, so that she too may become a living spirit resembling you males. For every female who makes herself male will enter the kingdom of Heaven.'"[6] Although the Apostle Paul is credited with saying that women are "saved through childbearing," which in some circles has been used to reduce women's spirituality to procreation,[7] the Gnostic Jesus came to "destroy the works of the female." In this statement the Gnostic Jesus does what has been done for centuries: connect maleness to what is spiritual and higher and women to what is lower. Nothing even close to this comes out of the mouth of Jesus in the four biblical gospels. For women, the Gnostic inward journey to spiritual knowledge requires a rejection of the material world and our female bodies.

In contrast, the early Christians believed in the goodness of creation and God's intervention in real history. Christianity, as a "fleshy" religion, understood the incarnation of God in Jesus as the highest affirmation of the body. The death and resurrection of Jesus, seen as a literal event, promised true salvation from humanity's greatest enemy: death. It wasn't merely spiritual symbolism. In our contemporary society, we have made death increasingly invisible—cleaned-up and sanitized so we don't feel the full weight of how death destroys human life. Throughout history, in societies riddled with frequent, early, and sudden death, it was much harder to sweep death out of sight. Instead of seeking to escape the suffering world, the early Christians believed in the coming transformation of this material world. The significance of the present world, along with the hope of a resurrection, gave them a theological basis for nursing the sick, rescuing abandoned babies (mostly female), and burying the cast-off bodies of the dead. In a pagan world busy appeasing angry gods, this body-affirming ethic greatly contributed to the rise of Christianity among women who had grown accustomed to enduring forced abortion, infanticide of their daughters, and obligatory marriages. The early Christian churches provided a shelter from brutal paganism. This body-affirming ethic remains at the core of authentic Christian spirituality.

The short-lived Gnostic movement was, unfortunately, able to win lasting influence, and some of its tendencies became embedded both in Christianity and Western culture. Throughout history it has taken a variety of forms, including body-denying practices, strict segregation between clergy and lay believers, and some forms of Christian mysticism. It shows itself in the tendency to overspiritualize and individualize the Christian faith. Gnostics' ideas are reflected in our overconfidence in knowledge as the way to human salvation. These ideas are also part of the currency of popular spirituality, which seeks freedom to explore without the confines of troubling dogma and makes the individual the ultimate source of spiritual authority. This results in a spiritually independent self that is in constant conflict with the community. This conflict provides the backdrop for the quest on the part of women to find God within.

My questioning of this individualistic viewpoint does not deny that self-knowledge and knowledge of God *are* deeply intertwined. Humanity has always felt the need to pursue self-knowledge as a way to attain wisdom. Philosophers as diverse as the Stoic Marcus Aurelius and ancient Chinese military strategist Sun Tzu spoke about the need for self-knowledge. Today, some find themselves on the Jungian couch, seeking to enhance self-awareness. Some explore new lifestyles: a dramatic career change, beginning or ending a significant relationship, or a whole-body makeover in the search for a more authentic self—a self that otherwise remains buried under religious guilt or social expectations. Coming to know oneself as a whole and knowing being is part and parcel of life's journey, and it is at the core of our spiritual motivations. We come to knowledge of ourselves and gain indwelling wisdom through a deep relationship with God.

A G-Spot

Acquiring self-knowledge is an important step toward living out of a deep-dwelling wisdom. People who don't know themselves will continually be plagued by double-mindedness and instability. They are very unlikely to live wisely or be reliable friends. For women, the journey toward self-knowledge is essential to becoming authoritative knowers. It is the key to overcoming our pervasive feminine self-doubt. Yet self-knowledge, like wisdom, is rather elusive. We can never gain the necessary distance from our own experience and point to ourselves by saying, "Here, that's me." We know the self indirectly. How we understand the pursuit of self-knowledge through an inward journey will determine how successful we will be at obtaining both self-knowledge and wisdom.

To gain self-knowledge is to become aware of our inner voice, which contains our motives, fears, desires, and unarticulated experiences. It has the potential to either reveal our God-given longings or beguile us with lies. Our feelings can clarify our values or fog our decisions. Contemporary philosopher Martha Nussbaum proposes that our emotions are, in themselves, value judgments on what we perceive as being in our best interest toward happiness and flourishing.[8] Self-knowledge is the process of clarifying this inner voice. Self-awareness begins with the recognition that my life is not a haphazard collection of choices and that my life can be lived in an intentional way.

It is this intentionality that makes us more than mere dust in the wind. Our intentions are most clearly exposed by what we do or don't do. Intentional living requires painful honesty to admit that our deepest-held beliefs are reflected in our actions—or to admit what our feelings betray. We daily make judgment calls about other people's behaviors, giving them meaning and attempting to decipher their motivations. But when it comes to ourselves, it's easier to make excuses for why there is a disparity between what we say and what we do. Knowing ourselves requires us to face our ultimate loyalties, our limitations, and our blind spots. It's probably the hardest thing we will ever do.

The hazards of the inward journey are many. We have to traverse multiple layers to see ourselves as we are. As we tunnel into our innermost rooms, what we find is not a naked, unashamed self. It's not a self-made confident woman or even an innocent child. Rather we find a self that is the sum of our relationships and experiences. We find our mother's daughter—a wisdom seeker who is disoriented by too many false messages. Instead of clarity, we find bewilderment. Inside ourselves we hear an echo chamber filled with the voices that make up our lives.

The experience of gaining self-awareness is mostly about coming to terms with a gnarly knot of contradictory desires. Torn between craving for excitement and the need for security, we give up chasing our dreams and hold on to a reliable paycheck. We may say we want to get married but talk ourselves out of the men who show up in our lives. Though we sense the need to be more fully connected to others, we can't manage to find the time. In a web of contradictions, singularity of purpose is hard to come by. Philosopher Søren

Kierkegaard wrote, "Purity of heart is to will one thing." Women in particular struggle with the idea of willing "one thing." The struggle is one between what we know to be true and our distorted need to maintain relationships at all costs. We are faced with our own feminine posturing, with its need to please and to accommodate social expectations. We are trained to base our identity on our ability to do emotional maintenance by remaining someone's good wife, dutiful daughter, or always-available friend. We risk losing our integrity by fighting to keep bad relationships at all costs. When we couch our words in safe language, when we hesitate to speak and act out of what we know to be true, we expose our duplicity. This keeps us from the singularity of purpose and the purity of heart needed for wisdom to take root in our lives.

It's this double-mindedness that reveals a lack of both self-knowledge and true wisdom. Jesus called it hypocrisy and could easily spot it. This made Jesus very good at parceling out intentions and applying a "hermeneutics of suspicion" to people's hearts. When a rich and powerful young man asked him what was necessary for life with God, Jesus responded by asking him if he kept the commandments. He said he did, but Jesus recognized his self-justifying attitude. Jesus challenged him by, in effect, saying, "If you are so scrupulous in your devotion to God to keep the whole law then it won't take much effort to sell what you have and give it to the poor." When the man heard this, he went away sad, because he was rich. Giving up his wealth for the poor wasn't something he intended to do for the sake of knowing God. His motivation to keep the law wasn't spiritual; rather, his motivation was to maintain his power in a world where keeping the law gave him a measure of respectability. Even spiritual and religious actions cover up other agendas.

Jesus saw the inward journey not as promising but as treacherous. As a Jewish sage, he affirmed what an earlier sage had written: "Truly the hearts of the sons of men are full of evil; madness is in their hearts."[9] To him, this insanity in the hearts of people was in need of transformation, not exploration. Our problem isn't merely our lack of self-knowledge but also our inability to change our delusional state. For Jesus, what is found in the heart—the inner self—is the source of all the violence and evil we see in the world. He said, "For from within, out of our hearts, come evil thoughts. . . ."[10] Jesus repeatedly warned us that our troubles, whether they be global injustice, hate, or lust for power, begin in the human heart. According to Jesus, a person's greatest enemies would be those nearest to her, those of her own house. Who is nearer to us than us? Jesus understood that our bent toward self-deception and self-betrayal would make the journey inward unfruitful.

People often quote Jesus' assertion that "the kingdom of God is within you" to validate their inner search for God. The implication is that Jesus is telling us to look to ourselves to find the answers for our life. Does this often-quoted line point to a "God spot"—a G-spot—in us? Is the kingdom of God within, or is the kingdom of God merely in our midst? Some scholars believe that "within" is an inaccurate translation from the Greek; "among" or "in your midst" is closer to the original meaning. This is more in keeping with Jesus' full teaching on the reign of God, which he depicted as a present and future state on earth in which justice and truth reigned. He continually challenged his followers to seek and to strive to enter this kingdom. Jesus, offering himself as the door to the kingdom of God, said, "Whoever believes in *me*, as Scripture has said, streams of living water will flow from within them."[11] It is the act of believing in Jesus that brings the reign of God and its wisdom, which is manifested among us, into our innermost selves. For Jesus, the inward journey would not give us wise answers; it was by entering into relationship with God that one could gain wisdom within. This inner wisdom would be a dependent wisdom, mediated by Jesus himself. Out of an engulfing experience of faith, the Spirit of Wisdom would come and dwell in our hearts. Only then would the kingdom of God truly be found within us.

The search for independent inner wisdom appeals to our contemporary sensibilities. This rings true, partly because life continually displays God's wisdom. There is a sense in which the wisdom that God has built into our frame is calling us. Inside and outside, we intuitively know when we are setting off on a bad course. The problem is that because we have been alienated from God since Eden, our ability to tune into this God-dependent wisdom seems to fade in and out like bad cell-phone reception. Our feelings change from one minute to the next. Our desires to be wanted and to be acceptable place us in a state of self-betrayal. We easily mistake the inauthentic for the real, only to later kick ourselves for it. We repeat the same mistakes over and over, losing ourselves in a relationship or finding ourselves again in a toxic situation. Repeated mistakes become life themes that we justify. In this way we become victims of self-deception and are unable to learn what our lives are telling us. Our desires and hopes were initially created to be a source of wisdom, yet our inner voice has become unreliable, making it hard to hear God's voice. No wonder self-doubt plagues us and wisdom is hard to come by.

An Inner Adventure

The questioning of the solitary journey as a reliable source of wisdom doesn't deny the need to experience God in deep, personal ways. Can we get away from the madding crowd to hear the voice of God anywhere? Is there room for a mystical journey? Can we experience wisdom residing deep within us? I was raised in a religious environment characterized, in part, by a strong skepticism of any emotional experience of God; we were encouraged to experience personal salvation but not to indulge in "vain imaginings" or emotionalism. What mattered was right action—piety. As I have had my own ecstatic experiences of the bliss of God, I have come to appreciate the subjective element in Christianity. How to reconcile these experiences and all the different strands of my faith has been my personal work.

Mysticism and the writing it has produced sometimes seem like disembodied and detached forms of spirituality, but Christianity is never an attempt to escape the world or the body. The development of the inner life isn't centered on self-actualization or escaping the confines of our flesh. The mystical appeal to the possibility of "divine union" needs to be understood in ways that remind us that we can experience deep intimacy with God, but we will never *be* God. We become more fully human, more creaturely. For me, this is a welcome relief. Being God is more than my small frame can bear. I have now come to regard the contemplative tradition, differentiated from a purely mystical way, as one of the best means of pursuing indwelling wisdom.

The Christian contemplative tradition includes a set of ancient practices that orients us toward God and continues the inward work of personal transformation. In my own search for wisdom, contemplative practices have come to be indispensable. When I have found myself perplexed by life and well-intentioned advice, pulling away into solitude has allowed me to hear what only God can say. It's the only way I know to be able to differentiate between good advice and social pressure, allowing true wisdom to emerge. The goal in Christian contemplation is not only a personal experience of the nearness of Jesus but also a reunion with God's people. By learning to be alone with God, I have learned how to be more open among God's people. Individually practiced contemplation returns Jesus to the center of our wisdom, allowing us to hear the wisdom in the community.

All the practices in the contemplative tradition help us become aware of the Divine in our lives. (It is beyond the scope of this book to explore all these practices. For those seeking to learn more, there are many good books on Christian contemplation based on centuries of experience.) It's through these ancient practices that we learn to integrate the wisdom of God into our own lives. These practices, among others, include different kinds of prayer, meditation on scripture, mindfulness, solitude, silence, and simplicity. Any one of these practices naturally leads to the others. Silence is a natural companion to solitude. Prayer goes hand in hand with meditation.

These practices can seem overwhelming to those of us who live hyperactive lives. They seem incompatible with our contemporary patterns of living. Nevertheless, I have found that, over time, mastering even one of these has made a significant difference in my ability to see and hear what God is doing. When I let them fall by the wayside, my feeling of spiritual disorientation increases, and my confidence begins to give way to doubt.

One form of meditation is the practice of *lectio divina,* or sacred reading, engaging us through attentive reflection on scripture. This slow and thoughtful way of reading scripture allows the time for us to come to a fuller understanding of the text and then respond to God. Whereas Bible study relies on the intellect, contemplative reading of scripture seeks to place the mind's imagination at the disposal of God. *Lectio divina* and the imaginative prayer method taught by St. Ignatius of Loyola are two of many methods that are centered on scripture.[12] By reading gospel stories attentively and thereby engaging our imagination, we have the opportunity to change our perspective. During sleepless nights this imaginative approach has allowed me see and hear Jesus say, "Peace, be still!" quieting my mind and soothing my ramshackle emotions. A slow, engaged approach to scripture allows mere scriptural knowledge the opportunity to become God's Wisdom in our hearts.

Not all contemplative practices require that we embrace solitude or that we become hermits. Mindfulness can be practiced in any setting. This particular practice has been invaluable to me, as I have learned to become more aware of the moments that make up the passing of an hour, the taste of a homegrown tomato, the abundance of wildlife outside my living-room window, and the movement of my body in an aerobics class. All of these require that I slow down my thoughts. It's nearly impossible to be mindful and pay attention while multitasking. It is possible, though, to integrate mindfulness, even in the presence of other people and everyday activity.

When my children were small and the days were filled with the commotion of life and work, I learned about mindfulness as I rocked them to sleep at night. Then I more fully understood these words of Jesus: "Come to me." Come and sit a while and rest. Mindfulness helps us develop an interior silence in which we can hear God speak through whatever is around us.

A more outward form of contemplation—of centering on God—is the practice of intentional simplicity. In a consumer culture it's quite a feat to refuse another gadget with its promise to simplify our life. By refusing the offers made by our consumer culture, we refuse to be defined by what we wear or what we drive. The more we possess, the more our hearts and minds are encumbered by the demands of objects that need to be stored, cleaned, and managed. The ancient sages regarded those who focused on the pursuit of things as having lost their hope in the future.[13] The wisdom of simple living allows us to understand that what we are and what we'll become is much more than the accumulation of stuff. Freeing our lives of clutter, inwardly and outwardly, increases our ability to hear God and decreases our responsiveness to the demands of the world.

In all these practices, Christian contemplation seeks to develop a deep inner dialogue with Jesus himself. This rich and varied tradition has been practiced across the centuries and has led many to a greater love for the world. It's fundamentally a personal work of reconciliation at the deepest levels of our souls. As we daily return to God as our source, we find ourselves newly reconciled to the community. To practice contemplation is to be continually reminded of our dependence on the mediated wisdom of God that comes to us through the community and scripture.

The practices of the contemplative life are at the core of the prophetic role. A deep, strong interior life is the fore-runner to truth speaking. As followers of Jesus, we have a prophetic role to play, when we remind ourselves and each other of God's words and actions. If we are to recover our voice in our lives and in the world, we would be wise to learn these spiritual disciplines. Jesus' own powerful work emerged out of forty days of silence and a solitary wilderness experience. He often broke away from the pressing crowds to go to a solitary place to pray. He encouraged his followers to pray in solitude, hidden from the eyes and ears of others.

Many biblical prophets encountered a time of solitude af-ter their initial call. These were lonely and perplexing times of questioning, waiting, and purging of the self. The wisdom of the prophets emerges from this solitude. Moses spent forty years in the solitary work of tending sheep before he effec-tively confronted Pharaoh to let his people go. Queen Esther spent months enclosed in a harem, preparing to approach the Persian king for the liberation of her Jewish people. Anna, a prophetess, spent decades in the Jerusalem temple engaged in her work of contemplation and prayer as she waited for the coming Messiah. She immediately recognized Jesus as the long-awaited Messiah because she had been listening for his call. The role of solitude in the prophetic tradition is in-structive. If we're to recognize the wisdom of God in the world and gain our voice, we'll have to pull away from our noisy lives and find much-needed solitude so we can cultivate the art of deep spiritual listening.

The role of scripture in contemplation is pivotal. The text—the narrative of God's redemptive history—orients our listening like a compass. As we learn to slow down and quiet our minds, we expand our receptivity. Our spiritual ears are open. We begin to hear Jesus say to us what he said when he healed a deaf man: "Be opened." In our crowded, propaganda-filled world, we need to be healed of our deafness to the voice of God. It is this deafness that renders us spiritually mute. To hear the voice of God provides us with power, not only to speak but also to act out of a deep knowing. The spiritual practices associated with the contemplative tradition move us toward this.

Over time contemplation changes how we experience the self. Our self-experience is entirely sensual and social, and is made up of our bodily feelings, passions, desires, and memories. As we draw near to God in prayer and meditation, our inner life, emotions, thoughts, and motivations become centered on Jesus. Our inner voice changes its cadence. The landscape of our emotions and thoughts is changed. As we enter the presence of God, we gain a distance from communal expectations and lose our self-consciousness. It is in this intimate relationship with God that we can come to know ourselves as *imago dei*—the image of God. The self becomes a mirror that reflects God's glory rather than the expectations of the world. In seeing ourselves as image bearers, we learn that "by your light we see the light."[14] In God's light of truth, humanity's relationship to all other created things is clarified. In this intimacy with God, there is no attempt to escape our sensual and social experiences; rather, they are placed in the light of God and seen in new ways.

Contemplation doesn't stop with our having gained our voice and recovered our *imago dei;* its work of reconciliation is not complete. Instead of locking us in our isolated selves, the experience of listening to the voice of God demands embodiment and a return to a wisdom community. Hearing God has a built-in requirement that the knowledge gained at the feet of Jesus must, in turn, become a lived wisdom. The faith encounter with God, as a self-defining event, radically changes the communal relationship.

This was true for both Hagar and the Samaritan woman. Their relationship to the oppressive elements of their life changed after they encountered God. Hagar found her dignity, and the Samaritan woman found her voice, as both returned to their communities. This personal encounter with God does truly allow us to both transcend and embrace the community. The follower of Jesus, in a sense, must first give up her dysfunctional community of origin, with all its false demands, in order to join the building of a new community of God's people. We first must break away in order to come home. Instead of coming home to ourselves, we come home to the embrace of other people who are also invested in God's love. They, too, are engaged in the daily work of reconciliation within their own hearts. Whenever we avoid the hard work of reconciliation, we need to be honest with ourselves about the ways in which we are contributing to the disintegration of the community—and that takes humility. Here, both the community and I are challenged and changed. In this mutuality, we can experience a true wisdom community.

A Sage Gathering

The search for self-knowledge and indwelling wisdom, free from the demands of a community or dogma, fits the contemporary desire for a free-floating spirituality. There are good reasons why this is appealing. We want to experience the feeling of belonging, of being at home, while at the same time we fear closeness to the sharp edges of others that a community naturally brings. Our communities, whether it's our family, our immediate circle of intimates, or religious or ethnic communities, are probably our greatest sources of pain. Many of us spend a lifetime getting over the hurts, small or large, suffered in our family of origin.

As fundamentally social creatures, we come to know ourselves only as we are known. We learn we are funny, kind, or intelligent by how others respond to us. It is through a particular and inescapable context that we learn to understand ourselves. Simultaneously, these same communal relationships trap us in definitions. Our sense of who we are, our purpose, and our destiny emerge within a particular community that exercises authority over this self-definition.[15] This is our problem. We know too well what it means to be defined by a community or a relationship that can be both unfair and cruel in its assessment of us, whether we are the pretty one, the smart one, or the odd one. To be told the essence of who we are, to be stripped of an authentic voice or action, is to be stripped of power. Yet the hope of connecting to God, ourselves, and the world is inescapably tied to a gathering of people. We are between and betwixt. Ultimately, we have to reconcile our longing for God with God's interaction with the community.

Many of us long for inclusion and mutuality within a wisdom community centered on Jesus. We are spiritually lonely, and there are too few places where the knowledge of God, the world, and ourselves can flourish. In everyday experience, this kind of faith community is as difficult to find as wisdom. The reality is that any gathering of Jesus followers lives in two worlds. One is the world of an emerging and future wisdom community, and the other is this present world with all its biases, power assertions, and messy history. Sometimes the wisdom community is readily recognizable; other times it's nowhere to be found. Then out of the blue it can show up unexpectedly. You can't go into a church building and be assured that you will find wisdom there. There are often too many conflicting agendas. An informal group of believers can have another set of problems, such as a personality cult or a disconnection from the historical community. Political infighting, longstanding personal conflicts, overbearing pastoral control—these factors and so many more rob our churches of the opportunity to become true centers of wisdom. Locating the semblance of a wisdom community is a continual challenge requiring a lifelong commitment, not only to finding it but also to helping build it. This means that we must take responsibility for the wisdom we have received from Jesus as we look for the wisdom community that is emerging in the midst of the world's conflicts.

The signs by which we can recognize a true wisdom community are the same signs given to the two disciples at the Emmaus gathering: the presence and centrality of Jesus, the focus on scripture, and the holy meal. Through the gathering at Emmaus runs a deep sense of being part of salvation history, of joining those who have gone before. A wisdom community always remains connected to its scriptural history and to Jesus as the Redeemer. Its commitment to the future is in making the Wisdom of God known to all sojourners by being open to new arrivals at its table. The wisdom community is a welcoming, life-giving, and self-challenging gathering of Jesus followers.

Here we face two problems in our search for indwelling wisdom and the community's role: the need to embrace the

Jesus of the gospels and the need to give up individual versions of Jesus and enter into the history of God's people by affirmation of the church's confessions—what it claims to know. A community that has chosen to follow Jesus knows what it knows, not through rational certainty but by an experience of faith. Here Christianity and contemporary sensibilities come to an irreconcilable clash. What the faith community claims to know seems to be at odds with our need for firsthand experience or scientific proof. Here we have to deal with what many view as troubling dogma—or worse. *Dogma* simply means authoritative teaching or doctrine, but we have come to view dogma as a belief held without adequate grounds, a mere stubborn assertion set up to exclude those outside its boundaries—one element in a political power play.

It's relatively easy to think of dogma only in the negative sense. I'm reminded of an overzealous youth who feared for my soul unless I accepted his specific dogma; never mind that I was already a follower of Jesus. In our radical individualism we have become resistant to the idea that tradition, community, and feared creeds should demand anything of us. What has taken its place is what Pagels describes as a search for the knowledge of God that is "beyond belief." This is a mystical knowledge that makes no claims and is rooted *solely* in our particular ethereal experience.

Honestly, does anyone live "beyond belief"? We all have a dogma, a set of boundaries, by which we pursue certain things and avoid others. We all have a particular wisdom, a pattern of meaning that we live by, even if we have not yet articulated it. Whatever dogma we have, we pass on to others because we believe it's the best explanation of reality. Of course, what is meant by "beyond belief" is that individual experience should take precedence over any communal claim. Yet to set belief or the community up against personal experience results in a false dichotomy. They are *both* necessary parts to a holistic type of knowing. Even as the heart responds in faith to the approach of God, the mind seeks to understand its reasons. None of us lives purely in experience. We all search to give words to the logic and true nature of our experiences. In this, the community is key. It is also true that even as experience needs an interpretative framework, we can't allow any confession, any claim to knowledge, to get ahead of our true individual experiences. Otherwise, our words are emptied of any meaning. This is the only way that we can move toward experiencing a holistic knowledge that captures our whole being, heart, and mind.

How do we deal with this issue of Christian teaching that many have come to regard as either unnecessary or exclusive? Can the confessions of the faith community be seen as something other than a door slamming in the face of would-be followers of Jesus? What are known as creeds and confessions of today are rooted in the earliest possible understanding of a historic faith community. Creeds and confessions serve as reminders of the bigger, fuller story. They are the *Cliffs Notes* of a sacred story.

In the 1940s, thinker and storyteller Dorothy Sayers eloquently expressed the idea that as far as the Christian faith is concerned, the "the dogma is the drama." The power of the Christian faith wasn't in the beautiful phrases, comforting sentimentality, or inspiring ritual; rather, the crux of the Christian faith was the drama-filled *story* of God, the Creator, becoming flesh in Jesus.[16] The "I believe" of the Apostles'

Creed reflects not merely an assertion of belief but also an articulation of a personal experience of faith.[17] It is the community's invitation to join and experience its story.

Ultimately, the true God can't be defined by our confessions. God is incomprehensible. We, however, experience God within a concrete world and a history to which our creeds bear witness. God is not limited by history or human language, but I am. Through embracing the confessions of the faith community, we walk into God's redemptive story to live in and through it. We join its wisdom. To be a follower of Jesus, to be Christian, is to join a sage gathering and its history.

In our desire for indwelling wisdom, we express the need for a knowledge of God that extends beyond merely accepting a set of propositions. We want the experience of God, not just an explanation. We're seeking a union of knowledge—true wisdom that can be lived. Christianity that is true to its roots doesn't reject experience in favor of a dry set of propositions to repeat mindlessly. Confessions alone don't impart knowledge of God. They aren't magical words, and they don't hold God. There is wisdom beyond what can be stated in creeds, and it is reachable only by faith. It is through the means of scripture, prayer, and sacrament that we are invited, not to simply repeat what was given to us but to experience the life of God. Entering into the hospitality of God is both a heart and mind experience—the Word made flesh in us. Only faith can complete the experience of God we seek. So when people object to "dead creeds," in one sense I agree with them. No one should repeat them simply because it's traditional to do so. Inattentive repeating of the creeds and participating in the sacraments may actually hinder the experience of their true meaning. Without faith they are nothing. Alone they have no life-changing power.

The call of Jesus—the Wisdom of God—is a radically different path from today's solitary inward journey. The assumptions are vastly different. The contemporary assumption is that whatever is wrong, it's up to us to save ourselves. Whether our problem is that we need peace of mind or we need a job, we are to find our salvation by solving the problem ourselves. Attempting to go outside the community, we believe that we can know ourselves by ourselves or with help of the right scientific tool or spiritual technique. We have come to believe that by exploring our desires and needs, we will become spiritually enlightened. The solitary inward journey promises the possibility that we can change the meaning of our experiences on our own. This therapeutic and solo spirituality demands nothing of the community and very little of us in terms of action. The world can simply continue unchallenged, oblivious to our needs, and we don't have to risk the exposure or change inherent in bumping up against the community. Wisdom is promised but never found.

The search for indwelling wisdom and the hope of becoming wise women requires that we be fully connected to our bodies, the natural world, scripture, and the community of faith. Unlocking these caches of wisdom remains dependent upon our faith in God, which grows through our experiences of God in the world. Knowledge of God is gained, not by an inward solitary journey but by faith that opens our eyes to the wisdom that is already in the real world we live in, with all its expectations, limits, and boundaries. As we listen in faith for the voice of Jesus, he comes and dines with us, feeding us his wisdom. His wisdom calls us to solitude, exposes our vulnerabilities, heals our self-doubt, and sends us out into the world. As we are reconciled to God and his people, we experience the joy of the deep-dwelling wisdom we seek. We then not only find ourselves but we also join the people of the world in looking for signs of God's Wisdom. In that way, we can continue to build the global wisdom community we hunger for.

Wisdom is justified by her deeds.

JESUS

7

PROPHETIC VOICES

W hen social activist and writer Dorothy Day died in 1980, many described her as the most influential Catholic woman of her time. Crowds of the poor and home-less came past her casket at her wake, grieving for the woman who had spoken for them. Because she identified with those who had become her community, she was buried in a plain pine box. Yet she may be remembered as one of the wisest women of the twentieth century.

What makes Day striking is that so much of her life was that of a quintessential, if ambivalent, feminist. Raised in a home with little spiritual nurture, from a very young age Day was on a quest. Her connection to God did not come sud-denly, yet it came through the natural movements of life. Her long search for an integrated and living spirituality took her from what she called a "shiftless" life of a radical socialist to a woman who founded the Catholic Worker—an international movement. In the process, she became the conscience of the wider church and a model of a wisdom seeker for our times.

As a young woman in the early part of the twentieth century, Day settled in New York City, working in the male-dominated profession of journalism at a succession of radical papers. Her coverage of stories increased her awareness of social problems hidden from the view of most people: the hungry crowds living in dank, smelly New York tenements, unsafe low-wage jobs, and the despair of chronic unemployment. What she saw firsthand, along with her friendships with communist, anarchist, and labor organizers, radicalized her. Her feminist passion for social justice propelled her to get involved in the women's suffrage movement. While picketing the White House on behalf of suffrage, she was arrested and served fifteen days at the Occoquan Workhouse, a Virginia jail facility. Ten of those days, she was on a hunger strike. Throughout her life, she was imprisoned seven times for nonviolent civil disobedience. Even so, her commitment to social causes never wavered.

Her participation in the sexual revolution of the 1920s meant that Day's bohemian personal life was as colorful as her career. She went from a series of affairs with men she met in the radical movements to an illegal abortion and a painful and brief marriage. By her late twenties she had settled into a long-term relationship with Forster Batterham. While living in her beach cottage on Staten Island with him—a man she truly loved—her spiritual center began to form. Batterham, a biologist and anarchist, shared with Day his love of nature, which in time became the basis for her spiritual awakening. It was through her sensual life and the intimacy of nature that surrounded the little cottage on the beach that she began to experience a deep hunger for God. Batterham didn't share her desire for God or her attraction to Christianity, yet in her autobiography, *The Long Loneliness*, Day writes of Batterham that "it was life with him that brought me natural happiness, that brought me to God."[1]

The sense of nature's wonder that kept Batterham an agnostic was, for Day, the entryway for her emerging faith. During that time, she experienced the joyful birth of her daughter, Tamar. This cocreative experience, with God and Batterham, sent her into what she described as an almost "mortal combat" for her own soul. As it has for many women, motherhood opened the floodgates of her spiritual longing. In one of her last public talks, she said, "My conversion began . . . at a time when the material world began to speak in my heart of God . . . of a Creator who satisfied all our hunger."[2] Her need to address the spiritual restlessness that had descended over her life eventually ended her relationship with Batterham.

In the summer of 1928, Dorothy Day was baptized into the Catholic Church. Her conversion was not without apprehension of the church's failures to address pressing social needs. Entry into the church didn't quench her desire to pursue social justice; rather, this desire was enlarged and redirected from a political ideology to Jesus' teaching to care for the poor and weak. Seeking to find a way to live out the social ethic of Jesus, she met Peter Maurin, a French-American street philosopher. Maurin advocated the significance of the person and relationships, works of mercy, and the rejection of institutional answers to human suffering that ignore the individual. The social ethic of Jesus was to be lived out through personal sacrifice, to be expressed through loving one person at a time. In 1933, creating a lifelong spiritual partnership, Day, as a single mother, and Maurin cofounded the newspaper, *The Catholic Worker.* Their first effort at publishing was small, with only 2,500 copies. The purpose was twofold: to increase awareness of the plight of the poor, unemployed, and homeless and to cast a vision for Jesus' social teaching.

For Day, it was not enough to simply write about the poor. She wanted to make it easier for people to feed, clothe, and shelter themselves. Day and Maurin embodied their ideas by establishing open-hospitality houses to take in the destitute and downtrodden on American city streets. Day, who was not a distant benefactor, made a commitment to live among the urban poor. Through her chosen poverty she sought to live out Jesus' words: "Watch out! Be on your guard against all kinds of greed; life does not consist in the abundance of possessions."[3] It was faith in the abundance of God that allowed her to practice voluntary poverty and identify with the people she served.

Over the next forty-five years, the workers and guests that joined her in the movement houses became her community of faith. This community was a salve for her chronic, lifelong loneliness. In her biography, she wrote about the loneliness of women: "We have all known the long loneliness and we have learned the only solution is love and that love comes with community."[4] Through the creation of houses of hospitality, Day not only provided for the needs of others but also found the antidote to her own sense of disconnectedness.

In the midst of this growing international movement, Day remained a contemplative person, reading the Bible and often praying for more than two hours every day. Through the discipline of contemplation, she learned to recognize the sacrament of the present moment. To her, Jesus' call to be part of his redemptive community was not some self-actualizing journey; it was a concrete, embodied way of life that began with Jesus as the center. Through an act of faith constantly repeated, she found Jesus and wisdom among the poor and unlikely. Day, as a laywoman, found the key to unlock the wisdom of God beyond the church walls.

This became her greatest service to the church. At a time when the institutional church was neglecting the social implication of Jesus' teaching, Day held it accountable through the eight books and hundreds of essays she wrote. The power of the pen and her way of life inspired others to see the woundedness of the world. Throughout her life, Day's faith-based pacifism and social-justice ethic propelled her involvement in a variety of social movements, from the antiwar movement of the 1960s to causes focused on gaining rights for migrant workers. Even after her conversion, her compatriots, as she described them, were the communist, atheist, and anarchist—the discontented of the world. These were the ones, she painfully acknowledged, who saw the Christian church as a hindrance to human liberation. She often quoted the theologian Romano Guardini's observation: "The Church is the Cross on which Christ is crucified."[5] Because Day lived out of what she had seen and heard and acted in faith, she became a prophetic voice, changing the way many people in the twentieth century viewed the issues of poverty and war.

Through her writing, as well as her chosen poverty and creation of a welcoming community, Day provided a prophetic voice for her generation. Her rejection of the conventional notions of American success, her suspicion of industrial capitalism, and her absolute pacifism made many uncomfortable. Because she was a complex character, Day's philosophy defied simplistic definition, which often led to misunderstanding. She was called a communist more than once; her critics accused her of being naïve, sentimental, idealistic, or just angry. Her life, undergirded by scripture and the faith community she fostered, became a glaring reminder that a life does not consist of the abundance of things, but of love.

I am not a Catholic, but as a follower of Jesus, I can claim Dorothy Day as my sister in the search for a knowledge of God that is made visible in our lives—wisdom. She lived out of a belief that faith must become action in order for us to truly know God and become wise knowers. Acting on her faith and being rooted in a community gave her otherwise fragmented activism coherence. She also understood that the natural world, the body, scripture, and the community all displayed God's Wisdom. As she began to hear the wisdom evident in the natural world and the body, it drew her to scripture and the community of faith. In her journey, she went from being a passionate but undisciplined radical, with just enough restlessness to keep from settling down, to a creative and powerful woman who affected the world in lasting ways. Through faith in God, she unlocked wisdom for her life and for the world.

THE ABUNDANCE OF MARY
OF BETHANY

Dorothy Day lived out in the twentieth century what the women who walked with Jesus had experienced. The wisdom he taught provided them the power to act and speak in the world. Their faith caused them to live out Jesus' words: "Wisdom is justified by her deeds." In doing so, they came to embody the knowledge of God they had received. Otherwise insignificant women who would have died in obscurity became knowers and proclaimers of God's love to the world. One of these women was Mary of Bethany.

The twelfth chapter of the gospel of John—an account corroborated in the gospel of Matthew—tells the story of Mary of Bethany. In the small town of Bethany on the eastern slope of the Mount of Olives (and just days before his crucifixion), Jesus was again found at a feasting table. Jesus had been in Bethany many times before. After a hectic three-year schedule of teaching and miracle working, a man Jesus had healed of leprosy—Simon—was throwing him a party. It hadn't fully registered with most of the guests or even his own disciples that this was a going-away party. They expected Jesus to do what he usually did at meals: teach them about the present and future reign of God. This evening it would be Mary, known as Mary of Bethany, who would teach this hometown crowd the lesson. She, along with her sister, Martha, and brother, Lazarus, was one of Jesus' closest disciples. All three had been invited to join the feast at Simon's house. Finding herself at Jesus' table many times, Mary had learned the art of deep listening and of recognizing the sacredness of the present moment. So she was prepared for this extraordinary evening.

While Martha was busy serving a scrumptious meal, Mary brought in a delicate alabaster jar, filled with a pound of pure nard. Nard was a very expensive aromatic oil from India; everyone knew to use it sparingly and only on special occasions. One of its uses was for anointing the body of the dead. Mary had saved this particular jar for a long time, waiting for the right occasion. This night would be the night. As Jesus reclined at the table, Mary broke the jar over the head of Jesus and let the ointment pour down his entire body, saturating his clothing. An overpowering musky, warm fragrance filled the room. The guests were startled, as we would be if an expensive bottle of wine were spilled at a dinner table. The response was understandable. What had Mary done? She'd made a mess, and the strong perfume had ruined a perfectly good meal. Was she crazy to waste all this nard? They had expected the honored guest to be anointed with oil, but a whole pound of nard—how extravagant! Indignant, Judas Iscariot, himself a thief and a hypocrite, rebuked her, saying, "Why this waste? It could have been sold for more than a year's wages and the money given to the poor." Hadn't Jesus advocated for the poor? The others joined in the disapproval.

While fragrance filled every room of the house, Mary quietly began to wipe the costly nard from Jesus' feet with her loosened, unveiled hair. Adding insult to injury, this was an immodest act for a woman in that culture, one that showed disrespect to the whole party. The criticism intensified, but Jesus responded, "Leave her alone, she has done a beautiful thing. Yes, the poor you have always with you, but you will not always have me. She did what she could and has prepared my body for burial." Mary is the only one who seemed to have heard what Jesus had been saying all along: "I will die. I will go away." The embodied Wisdom of God would not be with them much longer, and Mary had seen the urgency of the moment. The wisdom Mary had gained allowed her to see the true nature of this feast and to understand the significance of the days that lay ahead. Instead of a waste, her anointing of Jesus was the creative self-giving act of a wise woman.

Mary, like so many others, had experienced Jesus' words and miracles firsthand. But she had gone further; she had believed his words. The knowledge she gained had gone beyond hearing a sage's good advice or witnessing an entertaining miracle. By pondering and wrestling with his teaching, she had drunk deeply from his wisdom. In contemplating Jesus, she had learned to see herself and all things in the light of God. It wasn't just another spiritual fad; her faith in Jesus had allowed his wisdom to become part of every fiber of her being. The revealed knowledge of God offered by Jesus had become an embodied knowing, leading to the possibility that every act could be wisdom-filled. She had been so completely engulfed by this wisdom that this extravagant act felt as natural as breathing. She could not let this evening slip by without a demonstration of the love that was pouring out of her soul.

For Mary to engage in this prophetic act cost her something: she had spent considerable financial resources and let go of something she treasured. Facing social disapproval, she broke ranks with the other disciples and allowed herself to be thought of as an immodest woman. Acting out of what she knew and not out of what was expected, she displayed great wisdom. Mary nevertheless risked public humiliation. Without a word and solely through a simple act of love, she foretold Jesus' death and affirmed that he was worthy of worship. Because she was willing to appear foolish, she ended up displaying profound attunement to the moment. Jesus emphatically promised that wherever his message was spread, the story of that evening would be told in memory of her. Her extravagant anointing of Jesus became the supreme illustration of what embodied knowing looks like. In a culmination of the wisdom that had taken root, a simple, bold, and beautiful act became the monument to her life.

The risk taking that wisdom demands is possible because faith allows us to see the world, not as a place of lack but as one of abundance. Because of this abundance, Mary of Bethany could lavishly spill nard. Because of this abundance, Dorothy Day could embrace poverty. Wisdom's table of abundance allows us the freedom to forfeit power. We all have some form of power, whether it is social, political, economic, or relational. It may be our power that allows us to maintain relationships, climb the economic ladder, or gain influence. Wisdom is willing to risk all of this because it believes there is always enough. Wisdom isn't careless; it simply values what is truly significant and holds every aspiration and dream loosely.

To truly encounter Jesus is to see the abundance that he taught. Jesus told his followers to consider the wisdom of field lilies. They are both beautiful and content, never stressing out or worrying over how to flourish. Lacking the kind of power we value, they simply grow where they are planted. Their beauty is rooted in their dependency on the soil and the God-given sun and rain. To Jesus their beauty and wisdom exceed that of Solomon, a powerful sage king who lived in luxury. Because lilies illustrate abundance, we see that we, too, can give up power, divest ourselves, and flourish. Seeing the abundance they display denies that life is a zero-sum game. If we believe that there is only so much to go around, we hold on tightly to what we have and always strive to secure more of what is vanishing. If we believe in plenty, we are not afraid of suddenly finding ourselves without what we need. This allows us to take big, confident risks.

The Risk of Wisdom

Wisdom not only operates out a sense of abundance, but it is also bold. Unlike Mary of Bethany, who didn't exactly become the popular woman of the hour except in the eyes of Jesus, it's easy for us to imagine that being wise women means living on an ethereal plane, floating through life with a Mona Lisa smile. We tend to think that wisdom will cause us to be unhesitating in our actions and also gain for us the admiration of others because of our grace, serenity, and inner beauty. Our visions of life as wise women include living up to our potential while sipping lattes on a veranda. Self-confidence would ooze out of us, and our girlfriends would call on us and hold their breath to hear another one of our pearls. Our lives would assuredly be safe from doubt, failure, and social rejection. The bad news is that the wisdom of God isn't a safe and comfortable wisdom.

When I have been told to be wise, I usually take that to mean that I should play it safe. It means, "Don't rock the boat." This definition of wisdom is risk-free, placid, and compliant and mirrors the perspective of my friend Kerry, whose adult life has been dominated by her mother's need for safety—a need that makes it difficult to venture out into unknown territory. When Kerry was twenty-four years old and quit a job she had held through college, her mother's comment was, "Well, I guess you will never have any retirement savings." This small-minded view of life that operates out of fear of lack is never liberating. Now in midlife, Kerry's desire to change her life course is continually tripped up by this view of the "wise thing."

Is wisdom always the safe and conventionally prudent thing? Jesus was very good at overturning the conventional "safe" wisdom. According to Jesus, the wise thing to do is to lose your life, your power, and your dreams in order to gain your life. We, however, are told to plan ahead and take charge of our lives. Sometimes to gain our lives, we have to risk it. Conventional wisdom said that having moneychangers in the temple was good business; Jesus knew it was bad for people's souls, so he drove out the moneychangers and over-turned their tables with a whip—very unsafe. Conventional wisdom said you should defend yourself against false accu-sation and protect your reputation. Jesus refused to bring out his public relations machine. By breaking the Sabbath, going into unclean graveyards to heal a demoniac, and calling God "Father," Jesus discredited himself and was taken for a blas-phemer. In the eyes of those in power, Jesus was out of his mind. In stark contrast to what we expect, the Wisdom of God appears foolish in order to show us how to truly live as people freed from false expectations.

Wisdom is neither an abstract primordial truth nor a bunch of polite-sounding advice designed to produce a nice life. It's not a quaint list of do's and don't's. Like Mary of Bethany, true wisdom can often appear foolish, audacious, and reckless to a success- and consumer-driven society. In a life motivated by faith, wisdom may show up as a commit-ment to a work, a community, and a course of action that ap-pears self-limiting. It may limit us economically, keeping us from making as much money as we could. Wisdom may cause us to choose to live by different values—ones that make us the oddball among our friends. Wisdom may be reflected in the evaluating eyes of others, as they see us not maximizing our potential by being all we can be. It may call on us to give up being popular or considered a "good woman." For a person operating out of deep wisdom, this is not the result of low self-esteem; rather, it is a course of action freely chosen because she has experienced true spiritual freedom at Jesus' table. Instead of being a cozy accommodating life, following wisdom's path may actually make us feel as if we are putting ourselves in peril.

The singularity of purpose and integrity of wisdom may be more costly than we realize. For a person on wisdom's path, work, play, success, and even apparent failures become oriented toward disclosing the wisdom of God in the world. The true test of wisdom is in how we handle personal failure. It is not that we never fail; it is in how we respond to failed relationships, or to the realization that we've taken a wrong turn, or to the times of fog that inevitably settle over our lives. In all this, a person on wisdom's path seeks out the true nature of things—looking for wisdom between the gaps of events. In a life lived on wisdom's path, every moment speaks, and nothing is ever truly wasted.

Hearing Mary Magdalene

Another woman in the Bible who found wisdom in Jesus and responded wisely to the moment was Mary Magdalene. She has gotten much attention lately, with news articles, Web sites, and even worship services held in her name. You can attend the Church of Mary Magdalene and be anointed with oil and blessed in her name. This Mary is hot and the "it" girl of the moment. Her erroneous history as a weeping, repentant prostitute has given way to her depiction as the sacred bride of Jesus. A woman who was portrayed as a reformed prostitute and used as an example of a fallen woman for over a millennium is now (in movies, anyway) being viewed by those seeking a female savior as Jesus' wife—a woman who is awarded unlimited authority.

You fill in the rest of the story. There is so much myth, legend, and speculation about her that you may have to buy *The Complete Idiot's Guide to Mary Magdalene* in order to sort it all out. In an attempt to recover her story from centuries of misunderstanding, it's easy to overreach and distort her true role. In some circles, she has replaced Jesus as the symbol for Christianity and is considered its true prophet. In a post-feminist, post-dogma culture, she is a perfect candidate for our hungry spiritual imaginations.

There is no doubt that Mary Magdalene has been mistreated and miscast from just about every side. For over two thousand years, she has mostly been ignored. When I was growing up, she was very rarely mentioned, and when she was, it was always in passing. There always seemed to be a shadow over her. I just didn't know why. I didn't come to understand the significance of her role until much later, when she was one of the many women in Christian history I was trying to recover. Her significance is not in how much is written about her in the gospels, because there isn't much ink spilt for this Mary. Her significance is that she was a witness to the most important event that undergirds the entire Christian faith—the death and resurrection of Jesus.

The news of this singular event was first proclaimed by Mary Magdalene, though no one believed her at first. To understand why, we need to know a little about her story. The gospel writers say that Jesus had healed Mary Magdalene of demon possession. In our contemporary minds, it's hard to comprehend the idea of demon possession without thinking of *The Exorcist*. To put it in a way we can relate to, Mary Magdalene had been a mentally and emotionally tormented woman. Her life was one long sleepless night and agonizing day. Her malady rendered her voiceless; her credibility and her participation in the community was nonexistent. That by itself would account for why she wasn't believed, but that's not the whole story.

Once she was healed by Jesus, Mary Magdalene threw herself into his mission and joined his band of traveling theological students. She even supported his work financially.[6] Like the other disciples, both men and women, she heard his teaching and saw his miracles firsthand. She was captivated by how he made Jewish scripture come alive with parables instead of the dry dogma of the Pharisees. She gained firsthand knowledge of God by drinking deeply of his presence. Her days and nights of confusion were transformed and replaced with leisurely talks by the Sea of Galilee on warm summer afternoons, long walks on dusty roads hearing Jesus' vision of the coming reign of God, and many meals where she was able to take in the wisdom of his teaching. After a life of torment, her entire time with Jesus felt like one unending feast.

If anyone had a strikingly evident life change it would be Mary Magdalene. Jesus and the coming reign of God became the focus of her life. Jesus had saved her life by giving her a life; she joined his community and learned how to live. She evidenced her commitment and closeness to Jesus when she remained with him at the cross and accompanied his body to the tomb. When most of the disciples scattered in fear, Mary hung on.

Three days after the death of Jesus, overcome with grief, Mary was to be the first witness of the resurrected Jesus. Rising while it was still dark and packing her fragrant spices to anoint the body of Jesus, Mary ran to the tomb. She was dismayed when she found the tomb empty. As she wept inconsolably, Jesus, whom she did not recognize, asked her, "Why are you weeping? Whom are you seeking?" At first she mistook Jesus, who was hiding in his questions, for a gardener. Through a veil of tears and on the brink of hopelessness, Wisdom incognito almost eluded her until she heard that knowing, familiar voice call her name, "Mary." How could she not have seen him all along! He was alive. The first word out of her mouth was "Rabbi!" (teacher). This was her wisdom teacher. Jesus gave her a commission and a voice when he said, "Go and tell my brethren . . ." In this way, Jesus chose the very unlikely Mary Magdalene to proclaim his resurrection to the other disciples.

This story has been repeated so many times it's hard for us to grasp its significance. Mary Magdalene was a doubly unlikely witness—a former demoniac and a woman. Today, we also consider some people with a history of mental instability as unreliable. Like the women of her time and many others throughout history, Mary Magdalene wasn't considered a trustworthy witness—someone able to truly know. Jesus sent her anyway. Her story sounded like an old wives' tale to the ears of the incredulous disciples. In the eyes of the others, she, Mary Magdalene, of all the disciples couldn't possibly *know*. Her unstable past and gender made her a questionable witness, unable to perceive the truth.

Her wisdom in remaining close at hand, not knowing what she was anticipating, paid off. Jesus confirmed her story and established her credibility. From the first unexpected healing encounter with Jesus to a moment when she almost missed him, she went from being a completely discredited woman to being a truth teller sent by God. In her wisdom, she spoke out of her own personal knowing, regardless of whether she was believed or not. Remaining true to his instructions to her to deliver the news of a risen Jesus, Mary Magdalene went from a tormented silence to a proclamation that would resonate through the centuries. She didn't have to scream to be heard. By the third century, her role in the proclamation of the resurrection earned her the title of "Apostle to the Apostles"—a messenger of God to the sent ones. This is her remarkable legacy.

Mary Magdalene turned from her social voicelessness and spoke a message that would be heard across the ages. Mary of Bethany took a simple act of hospitality and brought it to life. Dorothy Day's lifelong spiritual search, with its uneasy and troubled spots, diffused great wisdom into the world. These women, whether in simple or grand ways, didn't hesitate. Through faith in Jesus, they acted from a personal sense of abundance and responded to the moment before them. Awakened to God by their own need, they recognized that the puzzle their lives presented was a gift of wisdom ready to be known. These women were willing to call things as they saw them and to live out of their own knowing—trusting what they had seen and heard. Through their words and actions, they showed themselves to be authoritative knowers and holders of wisdom. Without their kind of faith, the wisdom that is all around could be lost to us.

These women illustrate that Jesus wasn't (and isn't) in the business of creating docile women. Faith doesn't create passive women; religiosity does. Jesus is in the business of creating women and men who will carry his wisdom into the world, people who will bring out the wisdom of God that is already among us. Along with Mary of Bethany and Mary Magdalene, other women such as Mary of Nazareth, the prophetess Anna, and the Samaritan woman all experienced the transformative moment of recognizing the present movement of God. Encountering Jesus became their clarifying event. What they found was the path to God. Instead of echoing what they had inherited in their tradition and doing what was expected, they ventured beyond the confines they had known.

It is not just biblical women who can provide us with great examples. We can look at our cultural history and find others whose faith propelled them toward action and, subsequently, spread great wisdom into their worlds: abolitionist preacher Sojourner Truth, Salvation Army cofounder Catherine Booth, and social reformer Frances Willard, just to name a few. These nineteenth-century women dared to speak when it was highly unpopular and unconventional for them to do so. They demolished the expectations of what women could know and do. Even though we have greater—actually, unprecedented—freedom, I wonder whether our voices are any stronger than theirs. Our influence appears, at times, to be reduced to exercising our consumer power. For all these women, faith in God meant they had to act. Their faith wasn't merely personal and private; it had a public face. They could not remain silent or passive in the face of their encounter with God. Their spirituality had implications for their world.

What is conspicuous is that these women didn't have the privilege we have today, yet they were able to supersede their apparent limitations. Similarly, uneducated biblical women displayed the wisdom that can't be learned from books, picked up at a seminar, or deciphered in the esoteric. Feminine self-doubt, as a paralyzing feature of their lives, can hardly be found. What these women leave for us isn't so much their historical close encounter with Jesus or the causes that they championed but their willingness to speak and act in response to both the brokenness and the hope they saw in their own worlds. By doing this, they not only displayed the healing wisdom of God to the world but also became wise themselves.

Even when hesitation and double-mindedness is nipping at my heels, I have found comfort in these women's stories. I may have to go out of my way to find the stories and dig deeper into my faith, but they are there. I am not alone. Their lives can help illuminate my life. They have taught me that the desire to remain safe will never yield the kind of life I long for. The singularity of purpose and boldness saturated in love that we see in these women remains rare.

A Threefold Way to Wisdom

Unfortunately, it's easy to dismiss these women as somehow special, chosen. This is what bothers me about illustrations of women in seemingly extraordinary circumstances or times. Their stories can pass us by. In pondering these stories, I am left to wonder about myself, ready to make excuses. I haven't had the opportunity to follow Jesus around for three years. To me, Mary of Bethany can appear show-offy, stealing the limelight from other dinner guests and even from Jesus. Mary Magdalene was a little naïve to think she could ignore so many cultural expectations. Dorothy Day seems a little too austere for my taste. I'm not inclined to sell all my goods and live in a flophouse or take to the exhausting road year after year as a social reformer. I hardly vote, much less get arrested. I'm not generous with the abandon of Mary of Bethany, and I'm even less willing to risk public humiliation. I'm definitely not interested in opening my mouth if nobody is going to believe me. The muck and mire of too many better opportunities and choices can simply keep me paralyzed by inertia. I can think of a thousand excuses for why my life doesn't display their bold wisdom. Yet these women's stories defiantly stare right back at me. I have to be able to do something with these stories if their lessons are really going to matter.

Maybe what's tripping us up as wisdom seekers is the false promise that simply *seeking* knowledge will make us wise. If I just knew more about this or that, or if I gained more competence, I would be more effective. Our culture offers us the power of expertise—our own or someone else's. Decision making that relies on technique has replaced the true wisdom our lives and world need. But increased knowledge hasn't even resulted in personal transformation, much less the transformation of our world. We have more education than most women in the history of the world. We've already sat in too many seminars and paid for too many advisers. We're too smart for our own good, yet our painful need for wisdom continually shows up. The dissonance between the knowledge in our heads and the reality of our lives is desperately in need of healing.

The women we have looked at in this chapter found a path to turn mere knowledge about God and the world into an embodied knowing that is evident in their lives. This embodied knowledge produced lives of meaning, harmony, and great interior wealth. This path was laid out by the Jewish sages and taught by Jesus. Both the Jewish sages and Jesus understood that more knowledge didn't mean more wisdom; rather, an increase in knowledge can be painful because it points out the gap between what we know and what we live. This diminished and fragmented kind of knowledge—the kind currently dispensed to us—doesn't lead to wisdom. It doesn't teach us how to love, live in the moment, or recognize the abundance around us. Expertise doesn't produce courage, justice, or self-knowledge. In our contemporary, conflicted world, the divide between the intellectual knowledge we hold and true wisdom has increased.

The gulf between knowledge about God and our life is what the Jewish sages sought to bridge, even in their times. Because they saw Woman Wisdom—God's agent—at the very foundations of the cosmos, they advised their students to relentlessly look for her in everything. Because acquiring wisdom is the principle work of life, we are to sell everything and risk all, if need be, to find wisdom. There is an urgency to the sages' appeal to find a holistic kind of knowing that is lived out. There is an urgency present in our own lives to find wisdom. Created as wisdom seekers, we are compelled to seek wisdom out. Our bodies and souls are hungry for wisdom. The work of life, regardless of whatever else we may do, is to uncover this wisdom in every moment. This uncovering moves us toward a world where all will openly see the glory of God.

Where is wisdom found? The sages' Woman Wisdom stands "at the gate" and "beside the road." She first presents herself in our experiences. Wisdom is both in places of transition and standing on the sideline of our lives, waiting for us.

In Jesus' own parables, she hides in the perplexing, the contradictory, and the reversals. The underlying themes in our lives are her natural dwelling place. Her loud but faintly heard voice pleads for us to turn to her and pay attention. If we do turn our gaze toward her, in generosity she will enrich us. She will invite us to her table, offering the life of God. If we listen to her, our lives will no longer be haphazard collections of busyness but lives of meaningful action. We may be doing the same things we have always done—working, playing, relating—but their meaning and authority will profoundly change. In this way, we will gain an embodied knowing. At her table, we can know God for ourselves and become authoritative knowers and doers in the world. Pursuing her unleashes a healing power to a world in much need of wisdom.

The Jewish sages' threefold way of acquiring wisdom (nature, community, and divine encounter) remains a viable path for us. Through the observation of nature, they saw life as having a sustaining order. Yet, even as they expected an underlying order in the world, their worldview allowed them the openness to handle the parts of life that appear chaotic. By looking at nature they learned to see life as both orderly and baffling. Nature taught the sages to mindfully recognize that there is a time for everything. There are times when we experience such deep happiness that we don't want the day to end. There are other times when everything seems to be in a state of disharmony, with everything flying apart. We can't escape times of sorrow, pain, or wrong turns. Nevertheless, we can flourish in them. As much as we are told to plan for our futures, we can't really anticipate what is next. We can greet the moment, see it for what it is, and give it what it calls for. Pain, whether physical or emotional, acts as an alarm that something is wrong at a deeper level. Sometimes what is needed most of all is reflection, time out to really listen. Moments of great personal reversals can open up our hearts to greater wisdom. Our wisdom work is learning to listen for and dwell in these moments.

Nature not only teaches attentiveness to the moment but also reminds us of the abundance of the world. These two work in tandem. We can only attend to the moment if we recognize the world's abundance; otherwise, we would overlook the moment as we strive to secure our future. In one period of my life, when I was at a very low point and everything seemed to be falling apart, I experienced how nature can give us her present wisdom. Instead of the lilies of the field of Jesus, though, the illustration on this day would be cow patties. I was spending a weekend at a friend's Louisiana family farm, and I decided to take a walk—a good salve for emotional pain. On a sunny May afternoon as I walked through this old field, I noticed more than a few dried cow patties. I tried to avoid them, but grass that was already growing out of them made them difficult to see. Then I noticed that blackberries were abundantly growing out of some of these cow patties. It was an unexpected but delightful sight for a city girl. I began to pick blackberries right from the cow patties, carrying them in my hand until I had too many to hold. Then it struck me that even as my life at that moment felt like a cow patty, a pile of worthless refuse, nature's wisdom showed me that, even out of severe disappointment, fabulous abundance could emerge. This wisdom of the earth that revealed itself to me that afternoon provided an exquisitely beautiful moment of joy and hope. In countless other ways, nature reminds us of the abundance that is often both hidden and unexpected but always present in the moment.

Second in the sages' threefold path was the importance of the community in the acquisition of wisdom. In Proverbs, a son is urged to listen to the advice of his sage mother. Our mother—the community of faith—also provides us with guidance on how to respond to movements of the Divine in our lives. The community of faith provides the means by which we can name our experiences and give them meaning. In scripture and in history, we meet our partners in wisdom seeking. Across the centuries, stories on the pages of the Bible bind wisdom seekers together. Unwritten stories passed down through the generations provide a rich inheritance of tested wisdom. Our traveling partners in faith remind us that our wisdom remains always dependent on faith in God and that we can't acquire wisdom alone. Like a son looking to his sage mother, we can look to the Jesus community as a source of wisdom.

Last, it was the encounter with God that the sages believed ultimately defined the acquisition of wisdom. They saw the "fear of the Lord" as the beginning of and the grounding for wisdom. This fear is not what we imagine in our contemporary minds—a paralyzing estrangement; rather, the fear of the Lord is reverence and the conviction that God sustains all things. Under the eyes of God the sages gained confidence to live with ambiguity and perplexity. They didn't feel compelled to find an explanation for every inconsistency or to reduce the world to the controllable. The sages were not given to systematic theological arguments, and their often apparently contradictory writings can be frustrating to the contemporary mind. The belief that God's Wisdom was embedded in everything gave the sages the existential safety net that held their worldview together.

To succeeding generations of Christians, including ours, the Jewish sages' legacy of divine encounter points to faith in Jesus—the embodiment of Divine Wisdom. It's by faith that God's wisdom is made accessible to us. Faith allows us to recognize wisdom; faith also allows us to act on it. As we embrace faith as a way of knowing, it will put us on wisdom's path. This faith allows us to listen with attentiveness to the voice of God and provides courage to see the abundance that is already present. The sages' threefold and interrelated elements of nature, the community, and the faith encounter provide us with a road map for wisdom seeking.

In *The Road Less Traveled* author M. Scott Peck begins with this simple statement: "Life is difficult." The ancient Jewish sages were keenly aware of this. Their wisdom was not a Pollyanna version but was profoundly realistic. Wisdom seeking is difficult because, as Martha Nussbaum has written, "Knowing can be violent, given the truths that are there to be known."[7] What this means for us is that in order to live on wisdom's path, we will have to give up the illusion of safety. If we try to secure our safety, we will continually be doomed to dwell in fields of hesitation, stalled in neutral, forever wavering in the wind. As we seek to live in the tradition of Woman Wisdom—bold, clear, passionate, connected to God, and unabashedly unashamed—the wisdom present in the world will open itself to us.

As we follow in the path to God's wisdom, we begin, in small incremental ways, to affect our world. The world we start with is the one in closest proximity to us. Most of us spend our lives in the ordinary, with jobs, maybe even dull ones, families, grocery shopping. We may be severely limited by chronic illness, unwelcome circumstances, or a special-needs child. These are the worlds where knowledge can truly be transformed into holistic wisdom. Our lives may be cramped simply from saying yes too many times. Many of us haven't an inch to spare, much less room to think about unleashing wisdom in the world. But we don't have to take up other projects or venture far out of our everyday lives to be people who reveal the wisdom that God has infused into the world. Embedded in everyday life, Wisdom shows up incognito in ordinary ways. It is hiding in our work, our play, and our relationships and will be made manifest to us as we choose, by faith, to be attentive to what is already all around us.

Created as wisdom seekers, we are not made to live puny, uncreative lives. The process of wisdom seeking requires that we question not only the meaning and content of our work but also our lifestyles, our ways of relating, and how we choose to challenge the propaganda of consumerism and knowledge brokering. Some of us spend most of our work lives as lawyers, artists, teachers, or technology workers. Some are caregivers or do the invisible and often thankless work in homes and communities. What does this look like on a practical level if we're not trying to save the world but simply trying to get through the week? We can begin by questioning how we spend our days and the implications of everything we do. What are the interdependent consequences of my work, my relationships, my spending? How do I convert fragmented knowledge into holistic wisdom instead of simply acquiring more knowledge? We may not be able to control all the terms by which we work and live, but perhaps we can mitigate harmful consequences and even change some things. We may touch only a few lives around us. Wherever we find ourselves, wisdom seeking will require creativity, daring, and maybe even subversion that challenges our own conventional wisdom about what it means to be a woman in contemporary culture—and what it means to be wise.

The ancient sages used Woman Wisdom to make a transcendent God visible in everyday life. They knew that God's Wisdom could not remain remote and closed off if it was going to do any good. Even as the ancient Jewish people needed to see God's Wisdom near them, so do we. We don't have to settle for inherited traditions we don't own or that no longer resonate in our lives. A breathing and living connection to God is possible. By seeking God's Wisdom made fully manifest in Jesus, we can know God for ourselves and go from being merely wisdom seekers to wisdom bearers. By choosing to pursue wisdom, we choose to live the life of God now—a life filled with abundance, lived in the moment. Through this process we will not only know God but we will also know ourselves as prophetic voices. In our female life, with all its limitations and possibilities, we can reflect God's image and be the transformative agents of God's wisdom.

For the earth shall be full of the knowledge of the Lord as the waters cover the sea.

ISAIAH 11:9

8
FUTURE WISDOM

While making daily visits to a hospital intensive-care unit, I found myself writing this last chapter. Although it was a painfully difficult time, by the end of the ordeal I would see myself as a wisdom bearer for my father. It was also a time to see that God's wisdom comes to us unexpectedly and through multiple ways of knowing. In that realization I would experience a culmination of what I had written so far.

After two trips to an emergency room, my father lay in a small hospital room, attached to every medical device imaginable and growing increasingly unresponsive. He had been stricken suddenly with pancreatitis—a painful and ugly disease that created multiple medical complications. When my father entered the hospital, he could speak for himself, but over a two-month period, he became weaker and his silence became deafening. My father's illness gave me a profound, if unwelcome, opportunity to understand how wisdom appears in the messiest moments of life. The journey I describe in this book began with my questioning of my own knowing. Now I had to make life-and-death decisions based on that knowing. I no longer had any wiggle room. My experience with my father's final illness made it clear that I was a long way from where I had started.

My father's illness sent me into unexpected turmoil, as I was hastily drafted to play a role I had never imagined playing nor was in any way prepared for: to make the decisions regarding his care. With routine schedules shot, it became impossible to maintain any sense of normalcy. At first I felt lost and disoriented in the hospital's long, sterile hallways, facing a maze of medical jargon in the doctors' explanations of the disease. I turned to my own life-support systems: a cell phone kept me connected to my praying community; a Spanish Bible I had begun reading to my father reminded me that God's goodness and mercy were following me around the long corridors. Day after day, seeking ways to relieve my father's suffering left me exhausted. I craved sleep, but how do you sleep when your quivering soul is keeping you awake? What do you say to God when your mind is in a fog? Any prayer that I could possibly utter seemed wholly inadequate for the situation. Reducing life to the essentials, I prayed to be able to sleep, and I prayed that I could pray—the two things I thought might allow me to survive the days ahead.

From the beginning of my father's illness, the medical staff asked countless questions about his history. They gathered details, more than once, about the function of his body, his health habits, prior surgeries, and illnesses. Their questions were focused on a very narrow range of my father's experience. The goal was to gain control over the disease and his body's responses. In a peculiar way, the hospital was very egalitarian, using only a list of symptoms to differentiate one patient from another. My father's was simply one illness in a long list of illnesses this hospital would attempt to treat.

As he was shuffled among several specialists, there was an odd absence of questions about his moods or motivations. There was no interest in his background, attitudes, or dreams. The essence of my father's life was being ignored. I was left with the feeling that the knowledge of my father that the doctors had was insufficient for healing to take place. Couldn't they see that my dad was a gregarious and passionate man who was more than a medical history?

Before long, the complex diagnosis gave way to questions regarding his care. Do we perform the next surgery? In a likely sudden downturn, do we resuscitate? How much life support is too much? Facing the diagnoses of multiple doctors, charts, lab reports, monitors, gauges, and probes, it was I, as the eldest daughter, who shouldered the greatest burden regarding how far, how long, how invasive his care would be. Visions of a comatose Terry Schiavo and of the need for the "wisdom of Solomon" were hard to shake. End-of-life issues discussed theoretically as part of a sensational news story were now staring me in the face.

My father had left no written instructions addressing end-of-life decisions. It never occurred to him that life could possibly proceed like this; only by rummaging through memories of his life would I find the answers I needed now. It would be the innumerable conversations, shared meals, and life's travels that would provide the wisdom I needed. These memories couldn't be plotted on a graph. I had to rely on my intimate knowledge of my father and the faith we shared to yield the answer.

Philosopher Michael Polanyi proposed that we know *things* very differently from the way we know *people*.[1] The knowledge gained by dissecting a person, no matter how advanced the science behind it, is very different from that gained by living and sharing a meal with that same individual. It's the personal knowledge of others that allows us to love, hate, or empathize with them. And I knew my father; the doctors did not. In the hospital room, the tension between the knowledge the doctors were dealing in and the knowledge that I carried was palpable. Their first line of defense was to gain more information through another test; mine was to pray. Their goal was to fix his body; mine was for him to find wholeness. The gulf between these two types of knowledge had to be crossed in order for true wisdom to emerge.

In the middle of the science and technology that was being brought to bear on my father's body, another kind of knowledge was needed. The particular knowledge that became critical to his care couldn't be extracted by drawing blood. It had to be drawn from a personal understanding of him and his moods, motivation, and faith in God. It was up to me, and those close to him, to do the emotional work of sorting through his motivations and desires. I dove in, trying to learn the language of the place and to understand the medical diagnosis and treatment as best I could. Soon I found that, out of love, I was speaking for him, giving him the voice he had lost. With no relevant degrees, certifications, or titles—in other words, I was not an expert—I found myself advising, prodding, and influencing the medical process. As the days progressed, I saw how the valuable unofficial knowledge gave the medical staff a reference point from which to work. A mutual respect between the medical staff and me began to emerge. As medical knowledge, my personal experience of my father, and my faith in God came together, I believed wisdom would show up.

Along the way wisdom played peek-a-boo, as I continually was called on to make medical decisions. Each decision left me breathless, wondering what it all meant. Each time I found myself having to talk through the facts and my own intuitive sense of my father's wishes with those closest to me. Did I do the right thing? Would I be able to sleep that night? In the last few days of my father's life, I felt as though I were attempting to fly without a net. I couldn't rely on my own medical expertise. I had none. I couldn't rely on the medical staff; they had reached the end of their knowledge, displaying the limits of science. In the battle over disease, all of us found ourselves on our knees, waiting on the body's own wisdom, its ability to heal itself. The body itself would have the last word.

With no end in sight, the complications were mounting. In the face of narrowing options and higher stakes, I was awakened by the dreaded middle-of-the-night phone call. In a matter of a few hours, I would have to act in a way that would allow me to live with myself when all was said and done. After consulting with my family, I made the agonizing decision to withdraw life support. I made the same decision five times that night, asking the doctor to tell me the unsatisfying facts again and again, as I tried to relieve my sense of trepidation. No logic and no attempt to make sense of a senseless disease would ease my mind. What seemed inevitable to the doctor didn't seem so to me. I had to step out farther in faith than I ever have. Sustained as I was by faith in Jesus, God's wisdom showed up in that hospital; for a moment, in the depths of an ordinary night, in the midst of one of the most difficult decisions I've ever had to make, I had the honor of recognizing myself as a wisdom bearer for my father. At the end of my father's life, I could see that over the course of the two months he was in the hospital, I had lived as a sage, filling in the gaps between the facts.

My father's death left me with a profound and expected sadness. All the knowledge, love, and faith in the world weren't enough to fight off disease. Jesus' promise of a coming resurrection made my father's death nevertheless a hopeful one. For me there was also an unexpected sense of satisfaction, a deep confidence that I had been able to return to my father the sage wisdom he had shared with me during his life. I had struggled through sleepless nights to extract wisdom from the situation, and finally God's wisdom had appeared. There is no better feeling than knowing you acted and spoke out of your truest convictions. It's this sense of harmony and integrity that is wisdom's greatest gift. My life had come full circle.

MICROCOSM OF THE WORLD

It doesn't take much effort to see how my hospital experience parallels our lives in the larger world. Like the world we live in, a hospital is a vast storehouse of human knowledge accumulated over the centuries, tried, proven, and tested over and over again. The expert, the holder of this knowledge, is the authority. A hospital is today's most condensed version of what social critic Neil Postman calls a "Technopoly." He describes a Technopoly as a culture and an attitude that seeks its authority and takes its orders from technology.[2] As a microcosm of the world, a hospital resonates with all the complexities brought about by the cohabitation of technology and humanity. This world, which women have had less hand in shaping, tends to avoid seeing humanity in all its emotional and moral dimensions.

I wondered about the moral basis from which the doctors worked. However, I sensed that to bring this up, to acknowledge the presence of other factors in any significant way, would raise the existing ambiguity, the awareness of what is unknown, to intolerable levels and get in the way of their work. In the secular world, the most important human questions are avoided in the name of expediency. As my own experience shows, many times human experience can't be limited to the boundaries that science assigns.

The hospital, like the everyday world we live in, places human vulnerability in stark contrast with sterile attempts at exact answers. The inhabitants of our technician-driven world consist of two groups. There are the expert holders of authoritative knowledge—people whose performance is judged by their accuracy. The other group consists of those with broken bodies and lives, with no differentiating status other than a disorder waiting to be healed. The lines between these groups are blurred; we are all technicians, and we are all broken.

The medical staff, like all skilled workers, was trained to use scientific knowledge in the most precise way possible. Over time, I was able to see them as more than technicians applying their craft. I could see their struggle to maintain the cool demeanor expected of professionals and their attempts to manage their own curiosity and the feelings that naturally grow over time when treating a patient. Theirs was a battle to integrate what they could measure with what they felt. As individuals, they were like the rest of us—seekers attempting to find wisdom within their sphere of influence. Among these workers I saw a range of resistance and acquiescence to science and its machines: from the nurse who trusted her monitoring equipment more than the words of the patient to the nurse who found a way among the tangle of wires and tubes to remember the patient's humanity. To me the measure of the medical staff's competence—their wisdom—became the degree to which they allowed other forms of knowing to emerge.

The other inhabitants of this microcosm are the bodies of the sick. As in the larger world, our bodies and lives are messy, difficult to control. We are vulnerable to the ravages of disease and the sweep of circumstances, and we are in need of healing. Our God-given intolerance for suffering, our drive to live, and our creativity motivate us to discover the means for finding relief. The tools we create are one-dimensional, with one specific task—gaining control—whether the technology we use is a computer, a car, or a heart monitor. As my father communed with technology and became more dependent on it, his life seemed smaller. The lively music of his life faded to a mindless hum. It became a battle between the body's life and quickly vanishing dreams. As we submit our lives to the dominance of technology, mass media, and information, we may find that our dreams are whitewashed, standardized to fit the world. Under the viewpoint created by scientific rationality, we continue to create places where there are no personal dreams, no aspirations, no experiences to cloud decisions—just a march toward a predictable, soul-numbing sameness. Our subjective experiences matter to us, and we can never be comfortable with the attempts to standardize our lives. We continue to experience ourselves as vulnerable and tentative human beings for which the facts, the attempts at control, can feel inordinately cruel.

As we access the knowledge in humanity's storehouse, wisdom-seeking women and men have the opportunity to reshape it, to redraw its boundaries, to change its meaning and how it is ultimately used. We can create room for a holistic knowledge that integrates the diversity of personal experience, science, and faith. Wisdom will emerge when we are able to take this diversity of knowledge and create unity. By the transforming power of faith in Jesus—the Wisdom of God—human knowledge can be transformed into true wisdom that can heal our lives and world. The wisdom bearer for the task of transforming current knowledge into true wisdom will not be a technician but a sage.

Regaining the Sage Tradition

Today people sell expertise of varying quality, packaged in wisdom wrapping. They instruct us on how to eat better, work more efficiently, and reach our God-given potential. But we need wisdom beyond prepackaged and slick-marketed self-help guides and media provocateurs. Their distance from our daily lives makes any wisdom they may have difficult for us to access. We need leaders, teachers, doctors, lawyers, and caregivers who are *close* to us and are willing to venture beyond expertise to become people of wisdom. We need artists, musicians, and writers who are committed not only to their craft but also to the service of wisdom seeking. These are the sages for our time whom we desperately need.

What does a sage look like in our contemporary world? More important, how can we be prophetic sages in the varied places we find ourselves? In order to answer these questions, we need to understand what sages are and how they function. We have no contemporary category for them because sages defy categorization. Through faith and reflection, sages have learned to listen to the wisdom that resides in the body, nature, community, and scripture. They prod us to self-reflection as individuals, as families, and as a culture. The sages who have shown up in my life have most often done so unexpectedly. Because they listen more than they speak, they usually deliver one-line advice that adheres to the mind like super-strong sticky notes—but perhaps that adherence isn't immediate. Their teaching often escapes me at first; it's only through the passage of time that its true wisdom and its appropriateness for my life are revealed. Repeat the same advice to someone else, and it may not have the same resonance. Sages are the ones who incorporate faith into every kind of work, every experience, and every form of knowledge, transforming them into displays of wisdom. In this way, the contemporary sage has a personally and socially transformative task that is fundamental to creating a hopeful future.

Where do we find these people who are needed now more than ever? Sages do not necessarily write books, host talk shows, or take to the stage. They walk close to us and are largely defined by their presence in our lives, something neither the self-help industry nor the mass media can give us.

They are more localized, focused on the immediate concerns of people, uninterested in transcending what is close at hand. However, they may very well be hiding under the mantle of expertise. A sage may be hiding in an everyday profession. She may be a manager, an artist, or an insurance salesperson. Sometimes it's among the unsophisticated that sages live. Embedded in our institutions, they are largely unrecognized as sages by those around them. They are attached to the places that create our lives: a church, a school, or workplace. Like the ancient sages, who largely remained anonymous contributors to collected wisdom sayings, contemporary sages are often inconspicuous, fading into the background.

Sages, instead, teach primarily by their presence. Their knowledge is more diffused than an expert's. When she is hiding in a leadership position, a sage is best at finding the synthesis of order and chaos. She may be an accountant who not only knows the numbers but can also perceive the spiritual power of money in people's lives. He may be a teacher who is able to bring out in a difficult student her unique giftedness. Or a sage may be the friend who knows to deliver a casserole, even when we don't know we *need* a casserole. Sages go beyond theory, beyond method to a more holistic way of doing whatever they are engaged in.

Sages, as the nonexperts, draw from both the old and the new. They are rooted in the history and future hopes of a community. Their teaching is nonsystematic and more open to the exemptions—the things that don't fit in each life and situation they encounter. Instead of offering bottom-line solutions, they securely hold us up, as we remain on the precarious teeter-totter of life. Because sages have a great respect for history, they first appear conservative, yet their respect for accumulated experience should not be mistaken for a static view of the world. In fact, a sage may be more willing to break with conventional wisdom if it doesn't serve the flourishing of life.

Sages today can be the people who bring the biblical narrative and the faith community into a dynamic relationship with contemporary life. By fully engaging in the world, they act as reflectors, gently prodding the world to see itself and providing road signs for wayward travelers. They affirm forms of knowing that our world ignores. They are the ones who will first tell you that you are not crazy; they are naturally drawn toward the people who fall through the cracks. By combining multiple ways of knowing, they avoid the sterile answers to human problems. Sages are, above all, interested in real human flourishing, not in theories. In spiritual matters, sages are more interested in the quality of faith and how religious teaching serves that purpose. They are uninterested in endless theological arguments or empty rituals. Their primary interest is in living well by knowing God. The life they promote is no easy life, but it's a full life and a whole life. Looking at holders of wisdom in this way provides us with the possibility that any of us can act as wisdom bearers where we are. We may be the sage someone needs.

Jesus, the Sage, placed the key to the knowledge of God and wisdom in the hands of ordinary people doing ordinary things. He circumvented the established authorities to encounter people fishing, cooking a meal, or dealing in business. Wisdom would show up right there. Jesus said that those who become like little children would enter the abundant life of the reign of God. Children are the quintessential nonexperts in everything except faith and love. Their knowledge is simple, naïve, and rarely taken seriously. Historically, women have been in this nonexpert category as well; they still are in many situations and parts of the world. People who have a childlike attitude are the ones who will likely usher the reign of God into every nook and cranny of the earth. Some of the people Jesus encountered knew too much for their own good. Jesus didn't fit their interpretation of scripture. Their confidence in acquired knowledge set them up for spiritual failure. It is women and men who follow Jesus in a childlike faith who will finally catch up with Sophia. People who are on wisdom's path—the sages of our time—will usher in the reign of God. The sage, not the expert, will lead us into the future wisdom of human flourishing.

Sabbath as Wisdom Practice

Living as a sage requires a practice; the practice of Sabbath keeping, singularly and simply, captures the essence of wisdom seeking. For thousands of years, Jews, Christians, and Muslims have kept a rhythm of six days of work and one day of rest, following the pattern set by God. After the earth had been created in six days, on the seventh day God rested, establishing the Sabbath as the final crown of Creation—a feast. As a communal feast, Sabbath practice allows us the time to reflect on God's creative work. It places all our days and activities in light of God's work. The practice of Sabbath keeping in Judaism celebrates both Creation and liberation from Egyptian slavery.[3] In the observant Jewish home, the celebration begins Friday at sundown with a woman lighting the Sabbath candle. For the early followers of Jesus, the first day of the week—our Sunday—became a continual reminder of the resurrection and the hope of entering into an eternal Sabbath. Refraining from work and gathering for worship is a practice that simultaneously shows regard for the body, the earth, and the community in relationship with the God revealed in scripture. All the immediate sources of wisdom available to us are given a place in the Sabbath.

This is all good and well, but I remember the days of Sabbath keeping from childhood, and what I remember is a lot of wasted time. We went to church both morning and evening. Lunch was always my mother's spaghetti, unless there was a church potluck. Even if they did double-duty on Saturday to make the Sunday meal, women would still be the ones serving that meal on the Sabbath (I guess women's work wasn't really considered work). My friends and I often experienced Sundays as boring days that never ended. Nothing happened on Sunday. In Texas, with its blue laws, sidewalks were rolled up, stores were closed, streets were vacant, and even the public library locked its doors. If a heat wave was coming through, swamp coolers blew moist, cool air, helping us get through the day, but snow cones were unavailable on Sundays. To break up the monotony on special summer Sundays, we might get a watermelon or indulge in a water-balloon fight. In the winter, long naps broke up the day.

As I grew up, blue laws were abolished as inconvenient, and Sundays changed. We got busy. Stores remained open every day, some twenty-four hours a day; church became optional and then only in the morning. The hum of the swamp cooler was replaced by central air. A laboriously prepared Sunday dinner was replaced with takeout; we let someone else do the cooking. Naps were replaced with kids' soccer games. The old Sunday experience was all but gone.

What I didn't appreciate as a child was that on Sundays the pressure to achieve was off. Because anything considered work was avoided, it was a free pass not to accomplish a thing, and nobody complained if you lounged around. It allowed us kids the time to daydream, even as we passed the hours staring at the ceiling. I don't know if those around me ever observed Sunday with the proper Sabbath attitude of reflection. Jesus knew that people in his day didn't have the Sabbath attitude that the practice required—a radical attention to the community. It wasn't enough to simply avoid physical work. Sabbath for Jesus was a time to feast and heal. Jesus was bold enough to declare himself "Lord of the Sabbath," making the Sabbath the practical servant of Divine Wisdom.

Today, keeping the Sabbath takes all the resolve one can muster, partly because the activities of the other six days overflow into this catchall day. It quickly becomes the day to do that last load of laundry, shop for the coming week, or make lists for the days ahead. When nobody and nothing stops, it's easy to feel that you are getting behind. Because the Sabbath is foremost a communal feast, it's nearly impossible to practice it alone, so we let it slide. It seems that Jewish scholar Abraham Joshua Heschel was right when he wrote, "The Sabbath . . . cannot survive in exile, a lonely day stranger among days of profanity."[4] What we need is to get more Sabbath into our other six days so that Sabbath can breathe on its own. It's the cultivation of a Sabbath attitude every day that will make it easier for us to truly recover Sunday as a day to celebrate the gifts of God's Wisdom.

A Sabbath attitude flies in the face of classic economic theory, with its view of the world as one with unlimited needs and a chronic sense of scarcity. It's an attitude that says enough stuff and recognition has been extracted from our endeavors. Sabbath practice provides a built-in way for us to acknowledge our interdependency with the earth and others, recognizing them as gifts instead of means in our lives. By setting limits to our work every day and by abstaining from changing the world on the Sabbath, we practice giving up power. Things can be left as they are. In a world in which success is measured by how much we can get done, Sabbath allows us to opt out. Sabbath rest teaches us to trust that the work we do on the other six days will reach its purpose and completeness. We can enjoy nature, our bodies, and the community of faith through participating in word and sacrament. By foregoing the cell phone, we might even have time to daydream and find some wisdom in what is already around us. Maybe what God meant when he said, "Remember the Sabbath, to keep it holy" is to take time to remember the sources of wisdom that God has created. A Sabbath practiced as both a day of the week and an everyday attitude does exactly that.

Catching Up with Sophia

Like most of us, the world doesn't yet experience the wisdom of Sabbath rest. Humanity works feverishly to solve global ethnic, religious, and class conflicts, environmental denigration, and devastating diseases. From our individual lives to obscure places across the globe, our world is broken and exhausted. God's Wisdom is shut out by the increasing noise and activity of globalization. While knowledge in every discipline continues to increase at an accelerated rate, lack of wisdom is killing the world. Our scientific knowledge continues to outstrip our understanding of how to best use it. Theories don't do well in the hands of ordinary human beings, and there are glaring gaps in our knowledge. We can transplant a kidney, but we remain under the threat of another pandemic. We can talk across the world by phone, but we haven't figured out how to get clean water to all who need it. As we make the same mistakes and fight the same wars over and over, our experiences feel like reruns, refusing to yield wisdom for us. With all we know, we still haven't figured out how to have nations, homes, schools, neighborhoods, and workplaces that truly work. For many, the church still doesn't work. Every day we are promised a coming solution to a problem while three new problems are created. Nifty new answers open a Pandora's box of new complexities.

In our individual lives we have found that broken relationships and the plague of self-doubt will not be healed by therapeutic techniques. Living at peace with our bodies will not be attained by diagnosis alone. Our lack of self-knowledge and knowledge of God won't respond to another psychological test or religious seminar. We have turned to others who know better, and they have left us disappointed. Humanity is still looking for wisdom, and it still eludes us.

Instead of the promised future of science and technology, the biblical prophet Isaiah had a different vision of the future of wisdom. He saw a time when the earth would be saturated with the knowledge of God "as the waters cover the sea." This saying sounds rather nonsensical to us. The sea is, after all, water. How can it be covered by water? Even as the sea is the embodiment of water, everything will ultimately embody the knowledge of God and be wisdom-filled. According to Isaiah's vision, there will be a time of peace, harmony, and an unending Sabbath for both humanity and all creation. We who are suffering forgetfulness will remember the sources of wisdom. Once again, we will see the fullness of wisdom that is in the world. Reconciled to the wisdom of our bodies, the earth, and its creatures, we will find ourselves in harmony with the community and at peace with God.

This future wisdom will not be delivered by science but will be borne by women and men of faith who have encountered Jesus, on whom the Spirit of Wisdom rests. The knowledge of God that is to fill the earth includes the full participation of women as prophetic sages across the globe. Men and women will be co-knowers, living out the embodied wisdom of Jesus to bring *tikkun olam*—the repair of the world—to pass. Instead of a fragmented knowledge leading nowhere, there will be a union of knowledge, leading to true wisdom—an embodied way of knowing that yields harmony between the world and us.

The world is in need of restoration to all the sources of wisdom given to us by God in Eden. Jesus, by reconciling us to God, opened the way to the tree of life—the source of wisdom. The world is in need of sages—wisdom bearers, who, like Jesus, can face the propaganda machine of mass media, science, and false religion without flinching. Rather, they can disarm it of its overarching authority and become a redemptive force in the world. It is wisdom bearers who will take us toward a future that replaces the goal of rational certainty with the confidence of faith.

We have come full circle in our search for wisdom. We started out plagued by self-doubt, struggling to listen to our lives that were being drowned out by competing voices. Jesus has taught us that our feminine lives can reveal God's wisdom. God comes to us and encounters us in our everyday experiences. We, like Woman Wisdom, can live possessing our own knowing, firmly connected to God. Jesus taught us that we already know something that can lead us to God if we will simply pay attention. We can look to the mediated wisdom that is in the earth, the faith community, and scripture. We can give up looking to bankrupt authority sources and being isolated in our individual experiences. By faith, we can enter into a more powerful way of knowing that will yield wisdom for our lives and the world.

Like the serpent in Eden, the world continues to offer a source of wisdom independent from God. Jesus—the Wisdom of God—was unrecognized by the world; likewise, the Spirit of Wisdom that remains in the world today is largely unrecognized. It's this Spirit of Wisdom that is ready to help us unlock God's cache of wisdom, but it will take courage for us to confront the dominance of the world's knowledge systems. It will take courage to claim our own knowing, free from the dictates of experts. It will take courage to build a sage community that listens to the multiple sources of wisdom given to us by God. As we continue to follow Jesus—our Sophia and our Sage—we will discover that our search for wisdom ends with us—ordinary people acting in ordinary ways and in ordinary places, living as wisdom bearers for the world.

NOTES

Chapter One: Sophia Reawakened

1. Eller, Cynthia. *Living in the Lap of the Goddess: The Feminist Spirituality Movement in America.* Boston: Beacon Press, 1993, p. 48.
2. Kidd, Sue Monk. *Dance of the Dissident Daughter.* San Francisco: HarperSanFrancisco, 1996, p. 28.
3. Fonda, Jane. *My Life So Far.* New York: Random House, 2005, p. 551.
4. Daly, Helen. *Dallas Morning News.* "Talking about Mary Magdalene." Apr. 23, 2005, p. G6.
5. Eller, Cynthia. *The Myth of Matriarchal Prehistory.* Boston: Beacon Press, 2000, p. 2.
6. Christ, Carol. *Laughter of Aphrodite.* San Francisco: HarperSanFrancisco, 1987, p. 117.
7. Grenz, Stanley J., and Franke, John R. *Beyond Foundationalism.* Louisville: Westminster John Knox Press, 2001, p. 25.
8. Grenz, Stanley J., and Franke, John R. *Beyond Foundationalism,* p. 31.
9. Frymer-Kensky, Tikva. *In the Wake of the Goddess.* Columbine, N.Y.: Fawcett, 1992, p. viii.
10. Starhawk. *Dreaming the Dark.* Boston: Beacon Press, 1982, p. 9.
11. Exodus 19:9 (New International Version; used hereafter unless otherwise noted).
12. Heschel, Abraham Joshua. *God in Search of Man: A Philosophy of Judaism.* New York: Farrar, Straus and Giroux, 1983, p. 191.
13. Proverbs 2:6.
14. Wisdom is spoken of as a quasi-personification of an attribute of God. A hypostasis is an intermediate position between personality and principle. See Witherington, Ben. *Jesus the Sage: The Pilgrimage of Wisdom.* Minneapolis: Fortress Press, 1994, p. 109.
15. Frymer-Kensky, Tikva. *In The Wake of the Goddess,* p. 9.

16. Johnson, Elizabeth. *She Who Is.* New York: Crossroad Publishing, 1992, p. 87.
17. Witherington, Ben. *Jesus the Sage,* p. 12.
18. Heschel, Abraham Joshua. *God in Search of Man,* p. 92.
19. Witherington, Ben. *Jesus the Sage,* p. 50.
20. Matthew 13:11.
21. Matthew 11:19 (New Jerusalem Bible).
22. Luke 11:49.
23. Witherington, Ben. *Jesus the Sage,* p. 147.
24. Luke 15:8.
25. Witherington, Ben. *Jesus the Sage,* p. 375.

Chapter Two: The Intuitive Edge

1. "On the Move," *People,* Dec. 6, 2004, p. 98.
2. Witherington, Ben. *Jesus the Sage,* pp. 12–51.
3. Myers, David G. *Intuition: Its Power and Perils.* New Haven: Yale University Press, 2002, p. 1.
4. Lamont, Anne. *Bird by Bird.* New York: Anchor Books, 1995, p. 110.
5. Ehrenreich, Barbara, and English, Deirdre. *For Her Own Good: 150 Years of the Experts' Advice to Women.* Boston: Beacon Press, 1993, pp. 4–8.
6. Kluger, Jeffrey. "The Surprising Power of the Aging Brain." *Time,* Jan. 15, 2006, p. 86.
7. Woolf, Virginia. *A Room of One's Own.* New York: Harcourt Brace, p. 31.
8. Pagels, Elaine. *Beyond Belief: The Secret Gospel of Thomas.* New York: Random House, 2003, p. 183.

Chapter Three: Faith of Our Fathers

1. Ripley, Amanda. "Who Says a Woman Can't Be Einstein?" *Time,* Mar. 7, 2005, pp. 51–60.
2. Allen, Prudence. *The Concept of Woman: The Aristotelian Revolution.* Grand Rapids, Mich.: Eerdsmans, 1985, p. 66.
3. Stumpf, Samuel Enoch. *Philosophy History and Problems.* New York: McGraw-Hill, 1994, p. 47.
4. Allen, Prudence. *The Concept of Woman,* pp. 69–70.

5. Allen, Prudence. *The Concept of Woman,* p. 109.

6. Allen, Prudence. *The Concept of Woman,* p. 103.

7. Allen, Prudence. *The Concept of Woman,* p. 110.

8. Stark, Rodney. *The Rise of Christianity.* San Francisco: HarperSan-Francisco, 1997, p. 95. The reasons for this attraction were the rejection of female infanticide, forced marriage, and abortion.

9. Noble, David F. *A World Without Women: The Christian Clerical Culture of Western Science.* New York: Oxford University Press, 1992, p. 47.

10. Groothuis, Rebecca Merrill. *Good News for Women: A Biblical Picture of Gender Equality.* Grand Rapids, Mich.: Baker Books, 1997, p. 91.

11. Allen, Prudence. *The Concept of Woman,* pp. 414–417.

12. Allen, Prudence. *The Concept of Woman,* pp. 218–227.

13. Karant-Nunn, Susan C., and Wiesner-Hanks, Merry. *Luther on Women.* Cambridge: Cambridge University Press, 2003, p. 26.

14. Karant-Nunn, Susan C., and Wiesner-Hanks, Merry. *Luther on Women,* p. 29.

15. Karant-Nunn, Susan C., and Wiesner-Hanks, Merry. *Luther on Women,* p. 187.

16. Allen, Prudence. *The Concept of Woman,* p. 246.

17. Allen, Prudence. *The Concept of Woman,* p. 211.

18. Allen, Prudence. *The Concept of Woman,* pp. 214–217.

19. Allen, Prudence. *The Concept of Woman,* p. 418.

20. Allen, Prudence. *The Concept of Woman,* p. 413.

21. Allen, Prudence. *The Concept of Woman,* p. 443.

22. Allen, Prudence. *The Concept of Woman,* p. 110.

23. Bynum, Caroline Walker. *Fragmentation and Redemption.* New York: Zone Books, 1992, p. 68.

24. Bynum, Caroline Walker. *Fragmentation and Redemption,* p. 196.

25. Lerner, Gilda. *The Creation of Feminist Consciousness.* New York: Oxford University Press, 1993, p. 51.

26. Barger, Lilian Calles. *Eve's Revenge: Women and a Spirituality of the Body.* Grand Rapids, Mich.: Brazos Press, 2003, p. 62.

27. Bynum, Caroline Walker. *Fragmentation and Redemption,* p. 195.

28. Lanzetta, Beverly J. *Radical Wisdom: A Feminist Mystical Theology.* Minneapolis: Fortress Press, 2005, p. 100.

29. Bynum, Caroline Walker. *Fragmentation and Redemption,* p. 63.

30. Lerner, Gerda. *The Creation of Feminist Consciousness,* p. 77.
31. Bordo, Susan (ed.). *Feminist Interpretations of René Descartes.* "Descartes" by Karl Stern. University Park: Pennsylvania State University Press, 1999, p. 31.
32. Genesis 16:13 (New Jerusalem Bible).
33. Code, Lorraine. *What Can She Know? Feminist Theory and the Construction of Knowledge.* Ithaca, N.Y.: Cornell University Press, 1991, p. 50.

Chapter Four: It's in Your Bones
1. Tharp, Twyla. *The Creative Habit: Learn It and Use It for Life.* New York: Simon & Schuster, 1993, p. 64.
2. Barger, Lilian Calles. *Eve's Revenge,* 2003.
3. Berkouwer, G. C. *General Revelation.* Grand Rapids, Mich.: Eerdsmans, 1955, p. 117.
4. Psalm 104:24–26.
5. Psalm 19:1.
6. Allen, Ronald B. *The Majesty of Man: The Dignity of Being Human.* Grand Rapids, Mich.: Kregel Publications, 2000, pp. 137–138 (notes the interpretive work of Samuel Terrien).
7. Psalm 34:8.
8. Genesis 2:16–17 (New Jerusalem Bible).
9. Proverbs 3:11–18.
10. *Nelson Study Bible,* Commentary on Numbers 21:7–9. Nashville: Thomas Nelson, 1997.
11. Genesis 3:1 (New Jerusalem Bible).
12. Kimelman, Reuven. "The Seduction of Eve and Feminist Reading of the Garden of Eden." *Women in Judaism: A Multidisciplinary Journal,* 1998 (www.utoronto.ca).
13. Genesis 3:6.
14. Genesis 3:24 (New Jerusalem Bible).
15. Job 28:12–14.
16. John 4:5–42.
17. Walvoord, John F., and Zuck, Roy B. *The Bible Knowledge Commentary.* Colorado Springs: Chariot Victor Publishing, 1983, p. 285.
18. Frame, John M. *The Doctrine of the Knowledge of God.* Phillipsburg, N. J.: P&R Publishing, 1987, p. 65.

Chapter Five: *Memorias Vivas*

1. N. T. Wright believes this was a disciple and his wife. "The Resurrection and the Postmodern Dilemma." *Sewanee Theological Review,* 1998, *41*(2).
2. 1 John 1:1.
3. Jenkins, Philip. *Hidden Gospels: How the Search for Jesus Lost Its Way.* New York: Oxford University Press, 2001, p. 85.
4. Wright, N. T. "How Can the Bible Be Authoritative?" *Vox Evangelica,* 1991, pp. 7–32.
5. Brunner, Emil. *The Divine-Human Encounter.* Philadelphia: Westminster Press, 1943, p. 73.
6. 1 Corinthians 1:17–21 (New Jerusalem Bible).

Chapter Six: *Your Own Personal Jesus*

1. It is difficult to date Gnostic texts before the second century unless one engages in speculation. See Philip Jenkins's *Hidden Gospels: How the Search for Jesus Lost Its Way,* New York: Oxford University Press, 2001, for an overview of how these old texts are dated.
2. Pagels, Elaine. *The Gnostic Gospels.* New York: Vintage Books, 1979, Introduction xix.
3. Pagels, Elaine. *The Gnostic Gospels,* p. 54.
4. Jenkins, Philip. *Hidden Gospels,* p. 30.
5. Jenkins, Philip. *Hidden Gospels,* p. 211.
6. Patterson, Stephen, and Meyer, Marvin. *The "Scholars' Translation" of the Gospel of Thomas.* Polebridge Press, 1992 (verse 114 is found at www.misericordia.edu).
7. Jenkins, Philip. *Hidden Gospels,* p. 211.
8. Nussbaum, Martha C. *Upheaval of Thought.* New York: Cambridge University Press, 2001, p. 22.
9. Ecclesiastes 9:3.
10. Mark 7:21 (NIV Inclusive Language Version).
11. John 7:38 (NIV Inclusive Language Version).
12. See http://www.ccel.org/ccel/ignatius/exercises.xvii.i.i.html for explanation of St. Ignatius prayer method.
13. Book of Wisdom 2:1–9 (New Jerusalem Bible).
14. Psalm 36:9 (New Jerusalem Bible).

15. Grenz, Stanley. *The Social God and the Relational Self.* Louisville: Westminster John Knox Press, 2001, p. 305.
16. Sayers, Dorothy L. *Creed or Chaos.* Manchester, N.H.: Sophia Institute Press, 1974, p. 25.
17. Apostles' Creed: I believe in God, the Father almighty, creator of heaven and earth. I believe in Jesus Christ, His only Son, our Lord. He was conceived by the power of the Holy Spirit and born of the Virgin Mary. He suffered under Pontius Pilate, was crucified, died, and was buried. He descended into Hell. On the third day He rose again. He ascended into Heaven and is seated at the right hand of the Father. He will come again to judge the living and the dead. I believe in the Holy Spirit, the holy catholic Church, the communion of saints, the forgiveness of sins, and the resurrection of the body, and life everlasting.

Chapter Seven: Prophetic Voices

1. Day, Dorothy. *The Long Loneliness.* San Francisco: HarperSanFrancisco, 1952, p. 134.
2. Goy, Patrick G. "The Incarnational Spirituality of Dorothy Day." *Spirituality Today,* Summer 1987, *39,* 114–125.
3. Luke 12:15 (NIV Inclusive Language Version).
4. Day, Dorothy. *The Long Loneliness,* p. 286.
5. Day, Dorothy. *The Long Loneliness,* p. 218.
6. Luke 8:2.
7. Nussbaum, Martha C. *Upheavals of Thought,* p. 45.

Chapter Eight: Future Wisdom

1. Polanyi, Michael. *Personal Knowledge: Towards a Post-Critical Philosophy.* Chicago: University of Chicago Press, 1958, p. 343.
2. Postman, Neil. *Technopoly: The Surrender of Culture to Technology.* New York: Vintage Books, 1993, p. 71.
3. Heschel, Abraham Joshua. *God in Search of Man,* pp. 417–418.
4. Heschel, Abraham Joshua. *God in Search of Man,* p. 418.

THE AUTHOR

Lilian Calles Barger is the founder of the Damaris Project (www.damarisproject.org), an organization providing resources for women to start meaningful conversations in their communities. She is a native of Buenos Aires, Argentina. Prior to founding the Damaris Project, she had a twenty-year career in business and is a graduate of the University of Texas at Arlington. Currently, Barger works as a writer and frequent speaker on the intersection of the teachings of Jesus and contemporary cultural issues. She has written for numerous publications and is the author of *Eve's Revenge: Women and a Spirituality of the Body* (Brazos Press, 2003), which received outstanding reviews. She lives in Dallas, Texas, with her husband and two sons.

THE DAMARIS PROJECT

The Damaris Project is an independent nonprofit organization founded in 1997. Through a variety of programs it provides women with resources for starting conversations in their personal circles and communities about women's lives, culture, and the teachings of Jesus. We explore how spirituality informs our lives and work. The Damaris Project welcomes women of all faiths who are willing to explore life with us and to consider the teaching of Jesus in the context of women's culture.

For nearly 10 years, we have helped thousands to engage in exciting conversations in bookstores, coffee houses, homes, and on college campuses through public forums and the Damaris Salon[SM] small group discussion guides. To start a Damaris Salon conversation with your circle of friends contact us by visiting www.damarisproject.org for resources and opportunities.

INDEX

Paul, the Apostle, 79, 155–156, 168–169
Pearson, A., 63
Peck, M. S., 215
Personal propaganda, 63–66
Philosophers, women as, 81–85
Phoebe, 79
Plato, 75–77, 106
Polanyi, M., 222
Portia, 123
Postman, N., 225
Posturing, feminine, 48–51
Prayer, 177
Praying women, communities of, 90
Propaganda, personal, 63–66
Prophetic role, 180
Protestant Reformation, 80
Proverbs 1:20, 44
Proverbs 8:11, 70
Proverbs 8:30, 100
Proverbs 9:1–2, 132
Proverbs 9:5–6, 10
Proverbs 9:12, 2
Proverbs (*Meshalin*), 36

R
Rambo Jesus, 164
Rationality, 75–79
Reading, of Scripture, 151–152
The Red Tent, 28
Reformation, 80
Republic (Plato), 76
Resurrection, of Jesus, 134–138
The Revelation of Divine Love (Julian of Norwich), 86
Rice, A., 164
Risk, of wisdom, 201–203
The Road Less Traveled (Peck), 215
Robertson, P., 164
A Room of One's Own (Woolf), 69

S
Sabbath, as wisdom practice, 231–234
Sacred reading (*lectio divina*), 178
Sagan, C., 108
Sage gathering, 182–189

Sage tradition, regaining of, 227–231
Samaritan woman, 126–130, 182, 208
Samson, 150
Sarai, 96
Saraswati, 54
Sayers, D., 186
Science: and experts, 64–65; and wisdom, 234–237
Scorsese, M., 164
Scripture: and contemplation, 176–182; and Genesis, 112–122; as source of wisdom, 143–152
Self-doubt, 48–51, 81–85, 107, 171–176
Self-knowledge, acquisition of, 170–176
Serpent, in Genesis story, 118–119
Shakespeare, W., 123
Silence, 177
Simon, 197
Simplicity, 177
"Sisters of the Common Life," 88
Sistine Chapel, 112
Sojourner Truth, 208
Solitude, 177
Solomon, 53, 147
Sophia: in Gnostic Christianity, 54; and Jesus tradition, 32–42. *See also* Wisdom; Woman Wisdom
Sophocles, 53
Soul, significance of in Plato, 76–77
"Speaking," act of, 90–92
Spong, J. S., 165
St. Vincent Millay, E., 47
Stanton, E. C., 149
Starhawk, 31, 51
Steinem, G., 24
Subjectivity, role of, 92–98
Summa Theologica (Thomas Aquinas), 85–86
Summers, L., 71–73
Sun Tzu, 170
Symposium (Plato), 77